eBay

performance!

Selling Success
with Market Research
& Product Sourcing

by Robin Cowie and Jen Cano

ISBN: 978-1-4243-3915-0
eBay Performance! Selling Success with Market Research & Product Sourcing
by Jen Cano, HammerTap, and Rob Cowie, Worldwide Brands

Designed by: Richard Elton
Edited by: Steve Nye and Kirsten Overholt

Dedication

I'd like to dedicate this book to my wife, Sarah, and my amazing kids, Chantal and Peter. Thank you for always being there no matter how crazy I am.

—Robin Cowie

To Ramon, for believing that I can do whatever I say I can—and then pushing me to do it! And to Haley, Daniel, and Jacob for helping me make room for the living part of life every day.

—Jen Cano

Acknowledgements

This book is the result of 7 years of hard work – most of which was not done by me! Although I have been obsessed with the Internet ever since my last year of college in 1992, I began working at Worldwide Brands in January 2003 and it was only then I caught ecommerce and eBay fever.

This book would not be possible without the brilliant teaching, writings, and experiences of Matthew Hedges, Kirsten Overholt, Lisa Suttora, Janelle Elms, Sydney Johnston, Andy Jenkins, and most of all my business partner and great friend, Chris Malta. Chris started Worldwide Brands to help his fellow ecommerce entrepreneurs and over the 7 years of our company's history, he has touched the lives of hundreds of thousands of aspiring online entrepreneurs. Chris – I am greatly indebted to you for your wisdom and kindness. It is truly precious to find a human being who really cares about others' success.

I would be remiss if I didn't mention the wonderful guidance of my parents, Les and Fran Cowie, who not only taught me how to be an entrepreneur, but how to take life, like a snow globe, firmly with two hands and shake it as hard as I can causing a veritable explosion of joy every day.

—Robin Cowie

What a great journey this book has been! I could not have written about market research in such depth without the experience of numerous, real eCommerce businesses to draw on. Thanks to all our study participants. In particular, thanks to Tim Reynolds and Bryan Mills for opening your businesses to me and allowing us to share your learning experience with the world through this book.

I'm also grateful to HammerTap for providing an incredible team of bright and talented people for me to lean on during the creation of the book: Steve Nye for helping me craft the text for the book; Todd Wakefield, for making sure the calculations and formulas are accurate; Dan Long, for spending hours each week for the past year discussing with me new ways to use market research; and Greg Cole, for his counsel and fantastic vision.

And thanks goes to my husband, Ramon Cano, for so much support as I spent late nights and weekends writing this book. We went to school together, graduated together, work together, and raise a family together. This book is no exception.

—Jen Cano

Table of Contents

Introduction

In September of 2006, we sent out a call for participants in the popular Grow My Profits study. The study focused on how real-life businesses use market research and product sourcing, hand-in-hand, to build a solid online business foundation.

After careful deliberation, we zeroed in on qualified participants and went to work. Once a week, for 16 weeks, each study participant received one-on-one coaching from HammerTap and Worldwide Brands experts. Each study participant also submitted a weekly journal entry to help the team track their obstacles and their progress. Then, we all met together once a week to talk about what we'd learned. We tutored them and counseled them. They tutored us and counseled us.

The result was a startling look into simple ways to reduce risk and maximize profits in online businesses.

This book is the culmination of the insights we gained and strategies we developed during the Grow My Profits study. It is also the culmination of our experiences with over 100,000 aspiring online entrepreneurs and our combined 14 years of helping people answer two questions:

- What should I sell on line?
- Where can I get it for the best wholesale price?

Here, we share a specific method for offering in-demand products all the time so you can present your ultimate, lasting, and profitable eBay Performance.

As you read the book, watch for these symbols:

Analysis/Sourcing/Selling Tips: Read these for general information about how to use your eBay research tool.

Real-World Examples: Read these real-world examples of businesses that participated in our Grow My Profits study.

Quizzes: Take the quizzes to see how much you've learned or how well your gut-instinct is serving you.

Because Jen and I talk in the first person throughout the book, we have decided to use these two geeky graphics to let you know who's talking when.

This is my goofy picture. So whenever you see this, it is Robin talking.

This is Jen's tiny-bit-cooler picture. Whenever you see this, it is her talking!

Although both Jen and I collaborated on the entire book, Section 2 (largely based on research) is completely in Jen's voice, and Section 3 (mostly about product sourcing) is in my voice.

We hope you will find this book practical and useful for your business. Please don't hesitate to e-mail us your thoughts and results:

rcowie@worldwidebrands.com
jen@hammertap.com

Section 1

Lasting Performance with the Turnover Principle

"The Internet is just a world passing around notes in a classroom."

— *Jon Stewart, Interview in Wired Magazine*

How Captivating is Your Performance?

1

What do you have in common with a juggler? The same thing that makes her act successful, makes your product offerings successful, too. Let me explain.

Have you ever gone to the circus and watched a juggler? Just in case you haven't, let me share my experience with you. It really is fascinating.

Usually she starts out juggling three balls. Simple enough, right? "Hey, I can do that," you'll think to yourself—the first time you watch.

But, it never stays that simple. The juggler's accomplice starts tossing more items into the mix for the juggler to keep track of. Soon, the juggler is not only juggling three balls, but she's also got a couple of bowling ball pins and an apple that she's eating while she juggles. Now she's piqued your interest. You might stick around and watch a while longer.

Before you know it, the juggler is throwing and catching so many tricks-of-the-trade that your eyes have a hard time keeping track. She's got plates, forks, flaming torches, and knives. Now you're not thinking. You're just watching, completely amazed and captivated.

She's catching and throwing each item with precision. She's had the training to make it happen, she has a plan, and she's captivated you. By the time she's done, she could have been juggling a family of long-clawed, ring-tailed monkeys and it wouldn't have been any more amazing.

So, what does online retail success have in common with a juggler's success?

Simplicity.

When it comes down to it there is one three-step concept at the heart of successful juggling: release, anticipate, catch—1,2,3 and again 1,2,3 again. Simple, basic principles that are performed over and over—faster and faster—with increasing pizzazz—and simultaneously! A juggler adds a steady stream of items, new and interesting, to captivate her audience and increase the audience wow factor.

Three Steps for a Great eBay Performance

Just like in juggling, there is a simple, three-step principle at the core of online selling. This book is about that principle. Combining nearly fourteen years of ecommerce experience and interaction with over 100,000 small ecommerce entrepreneurs, we have teamed together to share our common experiences from the trenches of online warfare.

We'll use real case studies that illustrate how the most successful online entrepreneurs juggled to achieve success and how some of them simply dropped the ball.

Most importantly, we'll explain the importance of precision timing, knowing when to add a new product and when to get rid of an older product, how to anticipate what your buyers want, and how to deliver.

Simply put: **Research, Source, Sell**

We call it the Turnover Principle.

The Turnover Principle: Research, Source, Sell

2

The basic concept behind the Turnover Principle is that through it, you will build the basis for a durable, thriving business in a constantly changing market.

Here are the key benefits of the Turnover Principle:

Focus on Profit. You'll focus your attention on executing a flexible plan, rather than on reacting to unanticipated challenges. This means you can spend a majority of your time selling products that make a profit.

Stay In Demand All the Time. You'll have in-demand products on the market all the time because as you phase items out, you'll also phase new items in.

Stay Ahead of Change. Instead of being caught off guard with changes in demand, you'll know how to predict change and produce what your buyers want, when they want it.

The principle is simple. It's broken into three stages: Research, Source, and Sell.

For the principle to really work, you need products in all three stages at once: you need some that you are researching, some that you are finding sources for, and some that you are selling.

Research
Investigate to find out what sells and the profit you can make.

The Turnover Principle
Maintain Products in All Three Stages.

Sell
Sell consistently and stay ahead of changes in the market.

Source
Find products from reliable suppliers with maximum profit margin.

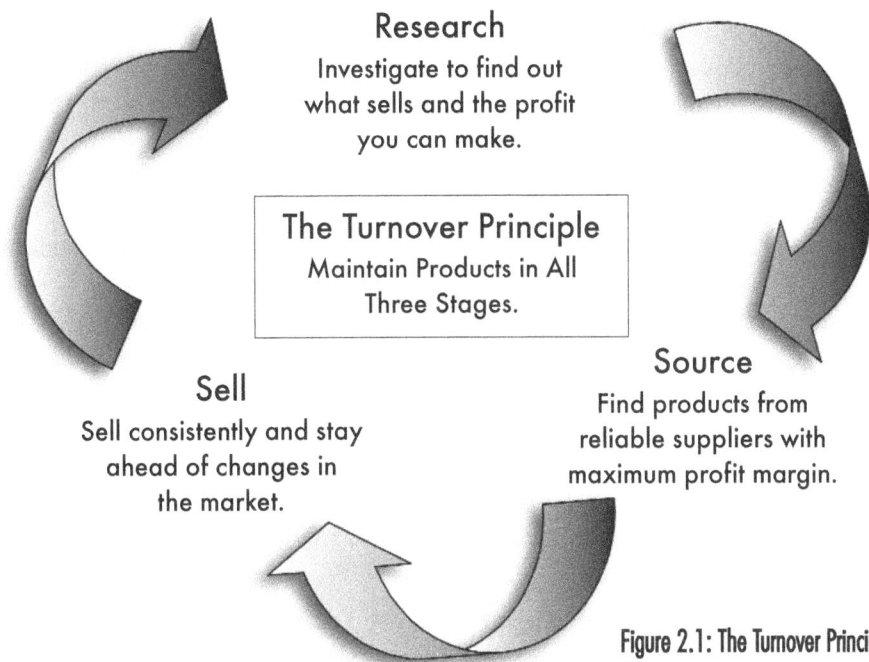

Figure 2.1: The Turnover Principle

When an item you're selling phases out, no sweat! You've been re-searching and sourcing other products to take its place. Your research, source, and sell cycle keeps revolving. 1, 2, 3, and again. See how it all fits together?

The best part—it's simple. And it will keep your business flexible, rolling with the punches, and way ahead of the competition. Again, best of all, this plan will help you pay the most attention to the products that will make the most money for you.

Let's take a closer look.

Research

The Turnover Principle begins with research because it reveals:

- What customers want to buy right now.
- How much they're willing to pay for "it."
- Whether you can make a profit on "it."
- Whether demand for "it" is rising or falling.
- The size of the market and your potential in "it."

Source

Once you've figured out what you want to sell, it's time to find a product source.

- Start with easy-to-use drop shipping to test markets and products.
- Use renewable sources to consistently deliver the right product at the right price.
- Grow your profit margin by using sourcing techniques that deliver larger profits.
- Offer a diverse product line that complements your primary products and allows you to cross-sell and up-sell.
- Use multiple product sources to optimize product mix, profitability, and flexibility.

Sell

Finding a reliable, affordable source for an item that will sell well on the market is a good start. Now it's time to follow through with a plan to maximize your investment and generate profit with no money left on the table. The keys to this phase of the Turnover Principle are efficiency and strategy.

- Start out simple, by selling smaller, lower margin items.
- Earn your customers quickly through loss leaders.
- Once you have customers, please them beyond their wildest dreams!
- Broaden your product mix.
- Get into trends early and monitor their progress.
- Up-sell, cross-sell, and add value.

A Profitable Cycle

See how smooth the process is? It's okay if you have questions or need more explaining, because we have the rest of the book to talk about the details of these three stages.

The rest of the book is divided into three sections—each correlating to one of the three stages in the Turnover Principle. These sections will answer your three top questions as an eCommerce business owner:

1. What do I sell?
2. Where do I get it?
3. How do I sell it?

Now you can see how similar this cycle is to juggling. As one ball is released, another is caught. The difference is, with your business, you are making a nice profit on each one of those balls, pins, knives and chainsaws!

Section 2

Research—What to Sell

"On the Internet, nobody knows you're a dog."

—Peter Steiner, cartoon in The New Yorker (5 July 1993)

Help Me Get Started—I Don't Know What to Sell!

3

Not everything sells. Not exactly earth-shattering news, I know. What might be surprising is that I can tell you how to figure out, without fail, what does sell.

In this chapter, Jen talks about:

- What makes a product hot
- Where to start looking for a product that's hot for you
- How to investigate and make decisions about specific products

Is it Hot or Not? Give it to me straight!

Let me tell you a little story. A year or so ago, a woman called me in a panic. She'd bought over $1500 in women's clothing and was having a tough time unloading them. With a garage full of inventory (and probably an unhappy husband) she needed help.

"How'd that happen?" I asked her. I soon discovered the problem. According to the list, the women's clothing category was hot. My friend based her decision about what to sell on that suggestion alone. She bought women's clothing... lots of it. But it wouldn't sell.

I've heard variations on this story dozens of times from novice and experienced sellers alike.

What went wrong? Four words: lack of focused research.

But this isn't going to be your story. Your story is confident. Your story is profitable. Why? Because after reading this chapter, you'll know how to find out what's hot for you and sell, sell, sell!

Move from Answering What's Hot to What's Hot for You

Hot lists, personal interests, pop culture, and advice from friends about what to sell definitely have their place. Let's face it. We don't live in a vacuum. It's important to take a cultural pulse and it's more fun to sell something you're interested in.

But, it can't stop there.

Remember that when you get general advice about a category, the advice is often based on averages. This means that some products in the category will perform above the average. But, many will perform below average. And where does that leave you? Let's just say you might not have room in your garage for that second car—you'll have left-over inventory in long-term storage, instead.

The point is, how will you know which side of the average line (above or below) your product will fall on?

Perhaps the most important step you can take toward finding products that perform well is to move from trying to find what's hot to finding what's hot *for you.*

Ways Hot Lists are Helpful	Ways Hot Lists Can't Help You
• Help generate product ideas. • Give general direction. • Point out which product types are performing well. • Identify categories that are experiencing growth over time.	• No information about specific brands, styles, colors, models, etc. • No information about how much other sellers paid for the item, and whether you'll be able to get the same price. (This is important for calculating profit). • Can't tell you what your profit potential is for the product (whether you will make or lose money).

To understand what I mean, you have to understand a little more about hot lists.

What's Hot for You? That's a Personal Question!

There's more to consider than just whether the product sells well and ranks at the top of a hot list. What's hot for another seller might not be hot for you because:

- Other sellers may have a product source you don't have.
- They might be able to get the product at a lower cost than you can.
- They might be able to carry inventory, while you need to drop ship.

What's hot is highly personal. And it depends on one thing: profit.

Your profit potential determines whether the product is hot for you or not. You can start investigating what's hot for you in a few ways:

- **Your Own Experience.** Try it out. If it doesn't work, try another product or another sales method. Keep track of what you are doing, and watch for trends of what works for you.
- **eBay's Seller Central.** eBay dedicates a lot of resources toward helping you understand how to sell better (http://pages.ebay.com/sellercentral/index.html). On Seller Central, you can learn about eBay buyers, hot categories, and specific categories and items eBay will be marketing over the next several months.
- **Market Research Tools.** This way takes trial and error out of the equation. Research tools will bring you, very quickly, from general ideas to specific facts about what is happening on the eBay marketplace.

Let me repeat: *your* profit potential determines whether a product is hot for you or not.

This means that no hot list, advice, or research can take your job. Your job is to make informed decisions based on what you learn from these tools. The more informed you are, the better your choices.

Your own experience is important. Hot lists will give you some good ideas. eBay's resources will give you a good sense of how to run an eBay business. And market research tools will arm you with knowledge about your specific buyers' wants and needs that you couldn't get anywhere else.

Market research tools lead you from general ideas found in a hot list, like "grandma slippers," toward more specific ideas, like "size 6 to 8 pink fuzzy grandma slippers with extra-soft insoles and built-in warming packs." With market research, you will zero in on which styles and models are selling best—and figure out what your profit potential is—in a relatively short time.

In other words, market research will lead you to discover *what's hot for you.*

Ready to try it out? You'll be amazed at what you can discover when you zero in on two small numbers: listing success rate (LSR) and average selling price (ASP).

Grow My Profits Study Example

The following journal entry is from Tim Reynolds, a Grow My Profits participant. When he wrote the entry, he was just beginning with the techniques I'm about to teach you in this chapter:

"Another thing that I haven't spent a lot of time on is looking at how products were selling in the past. I can see what products were big sellers last year and if other eBay sellers used any special techniques to increase sales during the holidays. A third thing I learned from Jen was how to find hot products, and keywords that I can use in my auctions to increase sales. These are all techniques that I will be testing this week."

How did he do? By the end of the study, through his use of research, his business showed a 40% growth in the last quarter of 2006 over the last quarter of the previous year (the Holiday season).

Highlights:
- Tim was a Gold PowerSeller during the study.
- Knowing which products to sell contributed directly to helping Tim earn 40% more revenue by the end of the four-month study.

Zeroing In
In the interests of keeping garage space free for your car (instead of unsold inventory), not to mention a lot of frustration and wasted money, let's begin narrowing down some specifics.

I'm going to tell you a little-known secret. Every single category, down to the very smallest one, has products that could be hot for you.

When you've had some practice, it will only take you a few minutes—ten minutes, tops—to figure out the hottest-selling products, with the best-selling prices, in any category. This is the process we're going to go through right now.

Let's say I have an interest in women's jeans, like the lady I told you about earlier.

What's the first thing we want to find out? In this case, we'll begin by figuring out the brands with the *best conversion rates* and the *best selling prices.*

(Stand up and stretch. We're about to get into the nitty-gritty.)

Phase 1: Investigating a Category

1. **Run a broad, category-level report.** In your market research tool, run a report on the narrowest category that fits what you're looking for. I've chosen "jeans" in the women's clothing category.

Figure 3.1: Category-Level Search

Figure 3.1: Category-Level Search

2. **Look at the overall LSR and ASP.** Write down the overall LSR (listing success rate), ASP (average selling price), and number of listings for that category. You'll use these numbers to decide which brands are better than average later.

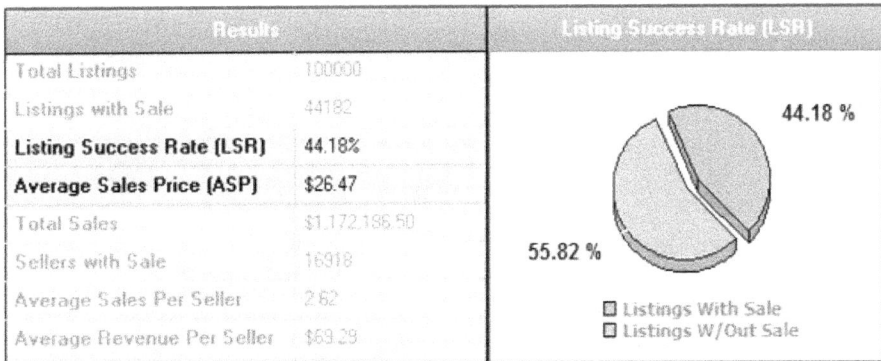

Results		Listing Success Rate (LSR)
Total Listings	100000	
Listings with Sale	44182	44.18 %
Listing Success Rate (LSR)	44.18%	
Average Sales Price (ASP)	$26.47	
Total Sales	$1,172,186.50	
Sellers with Sale	16918	55.82 %
Average Sales Per Seller	2.62	
Average Revenue Per Seller	$69.29	☐ Listings With Sale ☐ Listings W/Out Sale

(c) HammerTap, LLC. Feb. 10 to Feb. 16, 2007   ····:HammerTap

Figure 3.2: LSR and ASP for Women's Jeans

In my research for women's jeans listings above, I see that for 100,000 jeans listings, the LSR was 44.18% and the ASP was $26.47.

Not too bad so far, right? We've just discovered how much sellers make on jeans and how often they've sold.

3. **Write down brands with a great conversion record.** Scan the keywords in your research tool for words belonging to listings that sold. Some words will be part of listings that sold at a high percentage. This gives you an indication of what buyers are most interested in.

	Keyword	# of Auctions	Auction Success Rate ▽
3736	STRAUS	13	69.23 %
3737	SIZE16	13	69.23 %
3738	CHICOS	191	69.11 %
3739	MUSE	42	69.05 %
3740	319	29	68.97 %
3741	BRYANT	144	68.75 %

(c) HammerTap, Feb. 2007   ⋯⋮HammerTap

Figure 3.3: Keyword Analysis to Find Successful Products

For example, in the keyword analysis research example above (for listings that closed between Jan. 24-Feb. 23, 2007) notice that listings that had the word "chicos" in them sold 69.11% of the time. Chicos is a brand of jeans. And 69% is a fairly good conversion rate. So, I would write the word Chicos on my list. I would also write down "Bryant," another brand of jeans.

Write down the names of all the brands with the highest success rates (LSRs), along with the number of listings that included that brand (or styles, if brands are not appropriate for your search) in the title.

Analysis Tip: Beware of Insufficient Information

Another brand name, Straus, in Figure 3.3 performed well also. If you look at the Number of Auctions column, you'll see why. Notice that there were only thirteen listings (out of 100,000) that included the word Straus. That's just not enough data to base a decision on. With market research, be careful of making decisions based on too few listings.

4. **Write down brands with a great profit record.** Scan the same keyword report for the best selling prices. Write them down, along with the number of listings that included them.

Keyword	# of Auctions	ASP/Item ▽
SIZE 24X34	1	$169.95
SPADES	4	$169.47
DESPERADO	41	$167.80
CHLOE	18	$167.14
XL36	1	$165.00

(c) HammerTap, 2007

Figure 3.4: Keyword Analysis to Find Top-Dollar Products

Grow My Profits Study Example

During the study, Tim also learned how to evaluate products he was already selling, using the method I'm about to show you. Here's an excerpt from his journal:

"HammerTap has helped me to determine what to cut back on and what to increase...."

One important lesson we all learned from this study is that big change in profit doesn't always come from a life-changing revelation about what works really well. Often, positive change comes from understanding what doesn't work, and cutting that out of your business. This way, you can focus your time and attention on what is actually making you money.

For Tim, in addition to revealing what sells, research revealed the products he was marketing that weren't performing well across the entire eBay platform. He cut those out of his business and increased sales on products that he knew would sell. Here's the result in his words:

"My gross revenue is up over 40% since joining this study, the number of listings that I have has decreased by about 50%."

Highlights

- Often, positive change comes not from a life-changing revelation about what works really well. It comes from discovering what doesn't work, and cutting that out of your business.
- Tim grew from the lower end of the Gold PowerSeller limit to nearly Platinum PowerSeller during the four months of the study.

For example, in the research example above (based on listings that closed between Jan. 24 - Feb. 23, 2007), I can see that Desperado sells for an average price of $167. So, I would write that brand down on my list.

Hallelujah! Now you've got some more specific direction. In just four steps, you've learned about which brands (or styles, etc.) are in highest demand.

Take a moment to see what Tim Reynolds learned about this process during our Grow My Profits study on the previous page.

Phase 2: Investigating Specific Brands

Here are some of the brands I jotted down when I looked through the women's jeans category during Phase 1:

- Chicos
- NYDJ
- Hollister
- 7 for All Mankind

We're going to go through the process again. Only this time, let's look at information for specific brands to get narrower results. We know that these brands are hot, but what models, styles, sizes, etc. are really the hot sellers?

1. **Run a report on each brand.** In your market research tool, run a product search on each brand that you wrote down during your category investigation. In the research example below, I've run a report on 7 for All Mankind Jeans.

2. **Look at the overall LSR and ASP.** Write down the overall LSR (listing success rate), ASP (average selling price), and number of

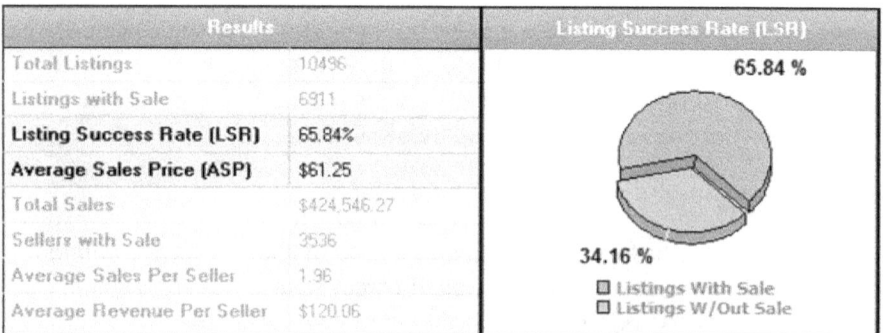

Results		Listing Success Rate (LSR)
Total Listings	10496	65.84 %
Listings with Sale	6911	
Listing Success Rate (LSR)	65.84%	
Average Sales Price (ASP)	$61.25	
Total Sales	$424,546.27	
Sellers with Sale	3536	34.16 %
Average Sales Per Seller	1.96	☐ Listings With Sale
Average Revenue Per Seller	$120.06	☐ Listings W/Out Sale

(c) HammerTap, Jan. 24 to Feb. 23, 2007.   ⋯:HammerTap

Figure 3.5: LSR and ASP for 7 for All Mankind Jeans

listings for that brand. You'll use these numbers to decide which styles or models are better than average later.

For example, in figure 3.4, the overall LSR and ASP for the jeans category was: 44.18% and $26.47 (see Figure 3.2). The LSR and ASP for 7 for All Mankind was 65.84% and $61.25 (shown above).

Comparing these figures helps you determine that this particular brand of jeans out-performs the average jean for that category. (Remember, that's why we want to get away from relying only on hot lists.)

3. **Write down styles/models with a great conversion record.** Now that you know that this specific brand is hot, you can find out specifically what styles, models, sizes, etc. are the hottest. Scan the research results for the styles with the best conversion rates (LSR). Write down the names of those styles, along with the number of listings that included that brand (or styles, if brands are not appropriate for your search).

Note: Use the same technique to find the best styles and models that you used to find the best brands during Phase 1.

4. **Write down styles/models with a great profit record.** Scan the same report for styles with the best-selling prices (ASP). Write them down, along with the number of listings that included them.

After you've written them all down, create a simple chart like this:

Brand	LSR	ASP	# of Listings
Chicos	70.39%	$17.43	635
NYDJ	71.04%	$51.31	922
Hollister	78.79%	$19.19	2857
7 for All Mankind	65.84%	$61.25	10,496

Table 3.1: Best-Performing Jeans Brands (Jan. 24 – Feb. 23, 2007)

With the information in a chart, it makes it easier to see which brand might give you the best return for you investment. Now you not only know the hot category (jeans in this case), but you also know specifically what jeans are hot.

As you make your decisions, bear in mind that each product and each brand is going to cost you different amounts. So, while the ASP for NYDJ is $51.31 and the ASP for 7 for All Mankind is $61.25, you still might end up making a greater profit with NYDJ than with 7 for All Mankind because of the price you will have to pay for the item.

? Quiz:

Are we ready to start looking for a source now? Why or why not?

Answer:

Not quite. We've done some good work. But, if you're willing to go through the process just one more time, you'll be ready!

Just like not every product in a "hot" category is hot, neither is every product for a "hot" brand hot. Remember, the numbers you've just looked at for brands are averages. The danger is that **some products will perform below average.** The great news for you, though, is that **some will perform above average.** And this is what we're about to find out!

Phase 3: Investigating Specific Products

This is the moment you've been waiting for. Just like on Family Feud when the host would shout: "Survey Says!" and all the answers would appear. Imagine how the contestants would have felt if they'd looked at the answers first.

That's how you should feel every time you investigate which specific products will sell before you ever invest in them. In our case, we have a list of specific styles, models, and sizes for each brand of jeans we found were hot. Now you can find out specifically. Here's how:

1. **Run a report on each style, model, size, etc.** In your market research tool, run a product search on each specific style, model, or size that you wrote down during your brand name investigation.

2. **Look at the overall LSR and ASP.** Write down the overall LSR (listing success rate), ASP (average selling price), and number of listings for each style. You'll use these numbers to help you decide the size of the market later.

Finished! You should have a table like the one below. My table shows best-selling styles for the brand of jeans 7 for All Mankind:

7 for All Mankind: LSR = 65.84%, ASP = $61.25

Style	LSR	ASP	# Listings
Low Rise	80.25%	$41.63	157
Boot Cut	76.33%	$42.45	207
Dojo	74.76%	$70.90	297
Pink Crystals	75.22%	$57.91	335
Stretch	71.66%	$60.07	561
NYD	72.44%	$90.20	508

Table 3.2: Best-Performing Styles (Jan. 24 – Feb. 23, 2007)

You might want to try out some combos like these, too:

Boot Cut and Stretch:
LSR=89.47%, ASP=$43.22
Low Rise and Boot Cut:
LSR=86.36%, ASP=$37.05

Look at those conversion rates!

Remember when I said that some products in a category would perform below average, while others performed above? Now you have no worries. You're not guessing. You know which ones perform above average in a hot category.

You're ready to begin gathering sourcing and pricing information!

Quiz:

If you had a source for 7 for All Mankind jeans, which styles would you select and why?

Answer:

Looking at LSR, every style of jeans listed here has a higher conversion rate than the average for 7 for All Mankind jeans at 65.84%.

Looking at ASP, you would say that only Dojo and NYD styles out-perform the average of $61.25. BUT this does not mean that the product is not hot for you! Even though Boot Cut jeans bring in $42.45 ($18.80 less than the average), they may be profitable if you could source them for around $35. Do you see my point?

A Word of Caution:

Unfortunately there are an increasing number of scammers on eBay, which you need to consider when you perform this type of research. Many people sell fake designer jeans and other products that sell for less than the authentic. Make sure you are comparing apples to apples when you do your research.

Grow My Profits Study Example

Tim Reynolds acquired the skill of quickly discovering which products are hot for him, and then aggressively moved toward finding a product source for it. His dedication to finding out what was hot for him was one of the foremost reasons his business grew so rapidly during the study.

Highlights:
- One of the first skills our study participants learned was how to identify in-demand products.
- I taught our study participants exactly the same method to find hot products that I have introduced to you in this chapter.

Is There Room for More Listings?

4

In college, my first minor was economics. But, the topic turned out to be… well, let's just say not my forte. As much as I didn't enjoy the nitty-gritty of economics, some important concepts did stick with me. One concept is:

The lower the demand, the lower the profit potential.
The higher the demand, the higher the profit potential.

That's a pretty simple one. Here's another important concept, which builds on the first one:

If supply is greater than demand, prices fall. If demand is greater than supply, prices rise.

During this chapter, Jen discusses:

1. What are supply and demand?
2. How big is the market for my product?
3. What's the balance between supply and demand for my product?

What are Supply and Demand?

I'm more of a multi-sensory learner, so I like to compare this concept to appetite. How much do you want to eat when you aren't hungry? Probably not nearly as much as when you are hungry. When there's a lack of food, you want to eat a lot. When there's an abundance of food, you're not very interested, right? It's easier for me to understand when I put it that way (probably because I'm a big fan of food!).

We've seen this phenomenon over and over again on the eBay marketplace. A hot new product comes out, with limited availability, and buyers bid like it's a life-and-death situation. Sellers make obscene amounts of money on those products—even though the public knows the product will be generally available in a matter of a month or so. When the product finally floods the market (increasing the supply and lowering the demand), the urgency to buy it decreases.

But these are dramatic examples. What happens if the balance between supply and demand is more subtle? With most products, you won't be able to guess what the supply/demand ratio is. You can't always guess if demand is low or high. And you can't always guess if there's more product on the market than is healthy for sellers. (Remember that we are trying to move away from guesswork through market research.)

More to the point: is there room on the market for more of the product you want to sell?

This chapter is going to help you solve that problem for your own business. Let your competitors try to guess, but you can direct your selling decisions armed with concrete knowledge about how hungry your buyers are for the product you want to offer.

What's The Size of Your Market?

What do I mean by the size of your market? I mean the dollars consumers are spending on your product within the eBay marketplace. I know—it's tempting to think that your market could be all of eBay. But, slow down Napoleon. You can still take over the world. You'll just have to do it one product at a time.

For example, let's say I want to sell angle drills . To find my market, I drill (no pun intended!) down into the eBay categories until I

Analysis Tip: A Case for Broad Research

For some research purposes, we want the search results to be based on a very specific product. But, for this purpose, we want to see what the size of the market is for all possible buyers. Sometimes, when you're doing this type of research, it's best to research an entire low-level category.

find the right one. In this case, it's: Home & Garden > Tools > Power Tools > Corded Drills > Angle Drills. You can see that not all of eBay is my market; just this specific category.

Overall Market Potential

Let's turn to research to find out the size of the market. After you've used your market research tool to run a report on a particular category or broad product (such as "angle drills"), it's time to look at three numbers:

1. How many total listings are there? (You may need to increase the number of results included in your listings to get the most accurate number.)
2. What's the total sales in dollars?
3. How much did each seller make on average?

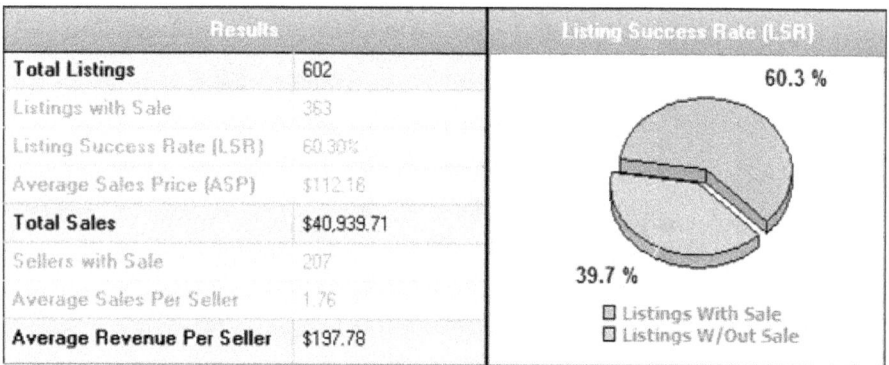

Results		Listing Success Rate (LSR)
Total Listings	602	60.3 %
Listings with Sale	363	
Listing Success Rate (LSR)	60.30%	
Average Sales Price (ASP)	$112.18	
Total Sales	**$40,939.71**	
Sellers with Sale	207	39.7 %
Average Sales Per Seller	1.76	☐ Listings With Sale
Average Revenue Per Seller	**$197.78**	☐ Listings W/Out Sale

(c) HammerTap, LLC., Jan. 27 to Feb. 26, 2007   ⋯⋮HammerTap

Figure 4.1: Total listings and Total Sales Reveal Market Potential

The results in the image above show us what the market looked like over a 30-day period. We can see that there were 602 listings, and that 363 of the listings sold for a total of $40,939, with sellers making $197 in gross revenue on average.

What this means is that the total opportunity for all sellers over the past 30 days was roughly $41,000. But the average seller only made $197. That information becomes particularly useful when you begin to compare the market size for this product against the market size for other products. Your goal is to find the products with the best overall opportunity.

Overall Market Potential vs. Top Ten Sellers

Now that we know what the overall market potential is, let's figure out who the competition is. I want to find out how big of a bite the top ten sellers have been able to take out of the pie within the angle drill market. I also want to know if it's going to be hard to compete against the top sellers.

To figure this out, we need to know:

1. How much did the best seller make?
2. What was the ASP per item for the top ten sellers?
3. What percentage of the overall listings do the top ten represent?
4. What percentage of the total revenue do the top ten represent?

Most eBay market research tools provide some information about other sellers. Below is a representation of the top ten sellers for the angle drill category.

Seller	# of Auctions	ASP/Item	ASP/Auction	Total Sales
1	47	$261.93	$277.34	$4,714.82
2	15	$239.99	$239.99	$2,639.89
3	5	$187.79	$187.79	$938.95
4	7	$129.29	$129.29	$905.05
5	4	$191.98	$191.98	$767.91
6	4	$169.95	$169.95	$679.80
7	3	$198.83	$198.83	$596.50
8	14	$137.49	$137.49	$549.96
9	6	$91.65	$91.65	$549.91
10	3	$183.17	$183.17	$549.50

(c) HammerTap, LLC., Jan. 27 to Feb. 26, 2007

Figure 4.2: Seller Analysis Tells Us about Market Potential for Top Sellers

From this, we can see that:

1. **Best Seller's Revenue:** The top seller (Seller 1) made $4,714.82 in the past 30 days. This is more than 10% of the overall gross revenue! Plus, there's quite a gap between this seller and seller number 2. This seller clearly dominates the category with 47 listings selling at an average of $261.93 each! This tells me that the potential to make a steady revenue stream in this category is definitely possible.

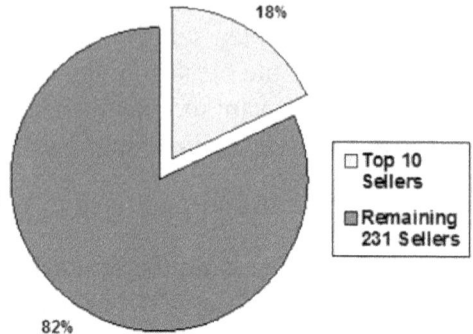

Figure 4.3 Percentage of Total Listings

2. **ASP for Top Ten:** The ASP per item for the top ten sellers was between $91 and $261. But, we can see that the majority of these sellers made $17 to $150 more than the overall ASP of $112 from figure 4.1.

3. **Percent of Total Listings:** The top ten sellers listed 108 of the 602 listings for this category. This is about 1/6, or around 18% of the total listings. (There were 241 sellers total). So, 1/6 of the supply for this category is coming from ten sellers. (See figure 4.3)

4. **Percent of Total Revenue:** The top ten represent about $13,000 of the overall $40,000 in gross revenue. That's around 30%.

Whew! Those are a lot of numbers.

But what does this all mean to you? Here's what it boils down to. The top ten sellers for this category are making a large portion of the money. But, the remaining 82% of all sales are being made by casual sellers, which are bringing in $27,000. This means that you, armed with market research, might easily be able to scoop up a large chunk of this 82% and $27,000 and become one of the top ten sellers in a hurry.

But what if the top ten sellers took up half the pie in sales and profits? This would mean that your market potential just decreased. It is much easier to compete with the casual seller because they rarely have great product sources and are rarely selling multiple items. So, the bigger the chunk not being eaten up by the top sellers, the greater market potential you have for your own sales.

But does it mean that there are enough hungry buyers on the market to make it worthwhile to you? We can almost say yes. But let's check on the balance between supply and demand before we make a final decision.

Quiz:
From figure 4.2, what else can you tell me about the top seller?
Answer:
We have already discovered that the top seller is dominating the market with total sales revenues of more than $4,700. But don't forget to look at the other columns, specifically # of Auctions and ASP/Item.

Now what do you find? The top seller within this market also has the highest number of listings, 47 (32 more than the next closest seller) and also has the highest ASP/Item, $261.93 ($21.94 more than the next closest seller).

If there was ever a seller you would want to emulate and try to beat out, it would be this one.

Balance Between Supply and Demand

This step is simple. You can find this balance with just two numbers: LSR and ASP.

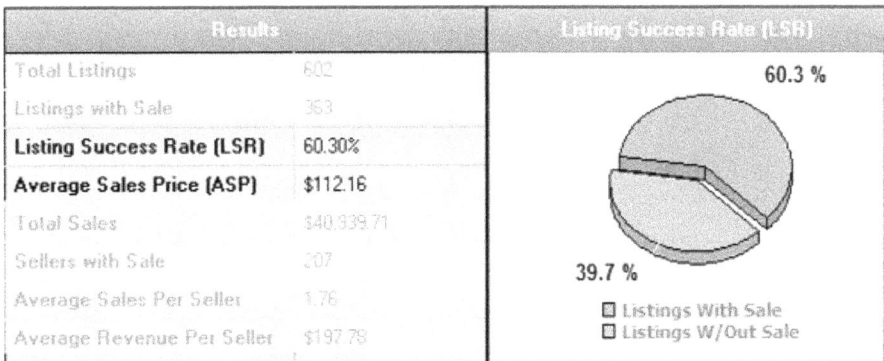

Results		Listing Success Rate (LSR)
Total Listings	602	60.3 %
Listings with Sale	363	
Listing Success Rate (LSR)	60.30%	
Average Sales Price (ASP)	$112.16	
Total Sales	$40,339.71	
Sellers with Sale	207	
Average Sales Per Seller	1.76	39.7 %
Average Revenue Per Seller	$197.78	☐ Listings With Sale ☐ Listings W/Out Sale

(c) HammerTap, LLC., Jan. 27 to Feb. 26, 2007   ····:HammerTap

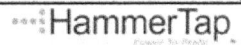

Figure 4.4: Success Rate and Sales Price Reflect the Supply and Demand Balance

The LSR is a literal translation of the supply and demand balance. It represents the percent of overall listings (supply) that were purchased (demand). In this case, 60% of 602 listings (supply) were purchased (demand).

The ASP is another indication of the supply and demand ratio. But, it's a little more subtle. If there is too much supply and not enough demand, we will begin to see this price fall over time. But, if there is not enough supply to satisfy demand, the price will be higher than the average retail for brick and mortar stores.

Room for More Listings

Let's get back to the original question: Is there room for more listings in this market?

We've discovered that there are a lot of sellers, but the top ten are taking away a huge amount of the revenue. And, of the top ten, one is completely dominant. This means that, other than the top ten, the rest of the sellers are most likely casual or weak sellers within this market (i.e., easy to beat). Also, only the top seller represents serious competition. This is the perfect opportunity for you to push through to the top ten.

We also know that six out of ten listings (60%) sell. Combine lots of weak competitors with a 60% conversion rate, and we have a winner! There's room in this category for another serious seller.

Grow My Profits Study Example

Often, sellers think the only reason to study the competition is to mimic what the top seller is doing. But, what if the top seller is no more educated than casual sellers about how he or she is listing? You're going to end up with only slightly better results.

Bryan Mills, a Grow My Profits study participant, learned important lessons about studying the competition during the study. His method was to understand where he was in relationship to the other sellers to find out whether there was room for his offerings (just like we talked about in this chapter). Once he understood his position in the market, how much more of the product the market would tolerate, and exactly how buyers wanted it, he was ready to dominate the market for that particular product.

At the beginning of the study, Bryan was offering around 107 listings a week—selling only 27% of them. Two months into the study, he was offering 38 listings per week and selling 48% of them. Great increase in success rate!

But, as always, we can't ignore selling price. Because of his ability to use market research to study the competition, Bryan's profits actually increased—even though he was offering only a fraction of the listings (38 instead of 107). He knew exactly what worked and, just as importantly, what didn't work.

I presented Bryan with the same information about studying the competition that I have presented to you here. He took that information and applied it to his business in meaningful ways so that he could spend more of his time on the things that actually made a profit.

Highlights:
- Bryan's business grew because he knew how to study his competition.
- I taught Bryan the same information about how to study the competition that I have presented in this chapter.

5

Is Demand Rising or Falling?

You can't fight gravity as long as you're on this planet. What goes up must come down. The problem is that we can't always tell if something is on its way up or on its way down.

During this chapter, Jen shows you how to determine if a product is on its way up or down! Learn how to:

1. Decide whether supply and demand are on the way up or on the way down
2. Understand the product life cycle
3. Develop selling strategies based on where the product is in its life cycle (even if it's a product you're already selling)
4. Predict seasonal increases based on last year's listings

Single Snapshots vs. Views Over Time

If you are looking at a photograph of a ball in mid-air, can you tell whether it's on its way up or on its way down? Probably not. A single frame in mid-motion will not tell you direction. But if you also had a picture of the same scene, taken just a split second before, you could compare the two pictures. You could see the direction of the movement, whether it was up or down.

The same principle applies with online sales, and we can compare the flight of a ball to the life cycle of your product.

When you are considering a product to sell, what happens if you just look at the product's performance at a single point in time? It's just like looking at the picture of a ball in mid-air. You can't tell if it's on its way up or down in its life cycle.

Every product has a life cycle. In the beginning, demand rises because of a lack in supply. At some point, demand begins to level out and balance with supply. Then, toward the end, demand falls and supply rises.

Going Up?

We're going to start this discussion with a quiz, based on the search results for remote control toy aircraft below:

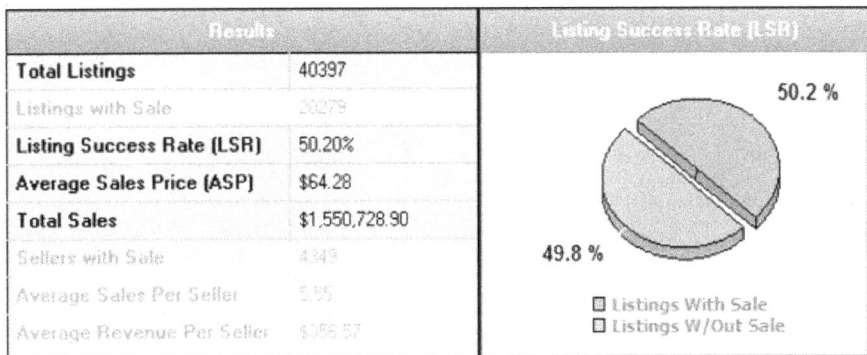

Results		Listing Success Rate (LSR)
Total Listings	40397	
Listings with Sale	20279	
Listing Success Rate (LSR)	50.20%	
Average Sales Price (ASP)	$64.28	
Total Sales	$1,550,728.90	
Sellers with Sale	4349	
Average Sales Per Seller	5.56	
Average Revenue Per Seller	$356.57	

50.2 %

49.8 %

☐ Listings With Sale
☐ Listings W/Out Sale

(c) HammerTap, LLC., Jan. 27 to Feb. 27, 2007.

····:HammerTap

Figure 5.1: Thirty-Day Snapshot of Remote-Control Aircraft.

Quiz:

Using the information in the research results in Figure 6.1, can you tell whether demand is increasing or decreasing? How about supply?

Answer:

I'm guessing you already know the answer. But, I'm trying to make a point. You can't tell whether it's increasing or decreasing because you are looking at a "freeze frame" of the market. Up to this point in the book, we've only discussed decisions based on single snapshots. Now, we're going to take several snapshots to look at a product's performance over time.

Determining whether a product is on its way up, steady, or on its way down is just about as simple as looking at several photos to decide the direction a ball is traveling. You do basically the same thing. Take snapshots of the product's performance at different points in time and compare them.

In this case, we're going to look at some snapshots, week-by-week, for the thirty-day period shown in Figure 5.1. Below are four snapshots for each week of the thirty days. Pay close attention to the bolded numbers:

- The total number of listings (supply)
- The LSR (conversion rate, or demand in sales)
- The ASP (selling price)
- The total sales in dollars (demand in dollars)

Week 1

Results		Listing Success Rate (LSR)
Total Listings	9328	
Listings with Sale	4342	46.55 %
Listing Success Rate (LSR)	46.55%	
Average Sales Price (ASP)	$63.97	
Total Sales	$337,869.23	
Sellers with Sale	1434	53.45 %
Average Sales Per Seller	3.68	☐ Listings With Sale
Average Revenue Per Seller	$235.61	☐ Listings W/Out Sale

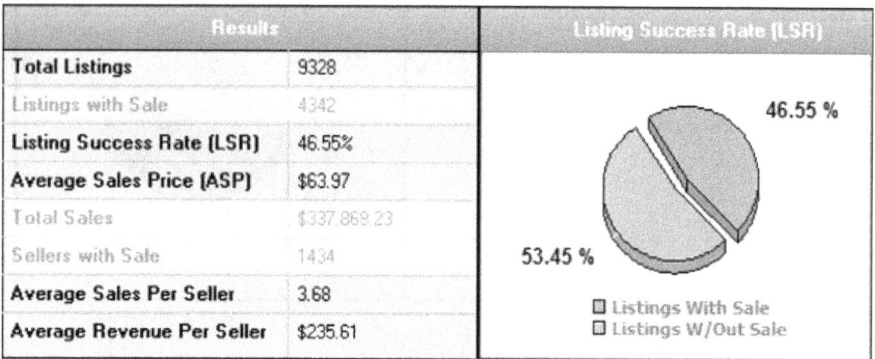

(c) HammerTap, LLC. Jan. 27 to Feb. 2, 2007.

····: HammerTap

Figure 5.2: Week 1 Snapshot for Remote-Control Aircraft

Week 2

Results		Listing Success Rate (LSR)
Total Listings	9218	
Listings with Sale	4417	47.92 %
Listing Success Rate (LSR)	47.92%	
Average Sales Price (ASP)	$64.26	
Total Sales	$337,798.86	
Sellers with Sale	1343	52.08 %
Average Sales Per Seller	3.91	☐ Listings With Sale
Average Revenue Per Seller	$251.53	☐ Listings W/Out Sale

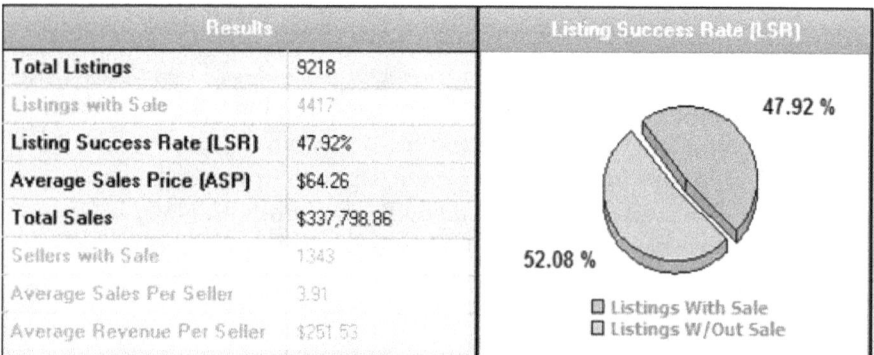

(c) HammerTap, LLC., Feb. 3 to Feb. 9, 2007.

····: HammerTap

Figure 5.3: Week 2 Snapshot for Remote-Control Aircraft

Week 3

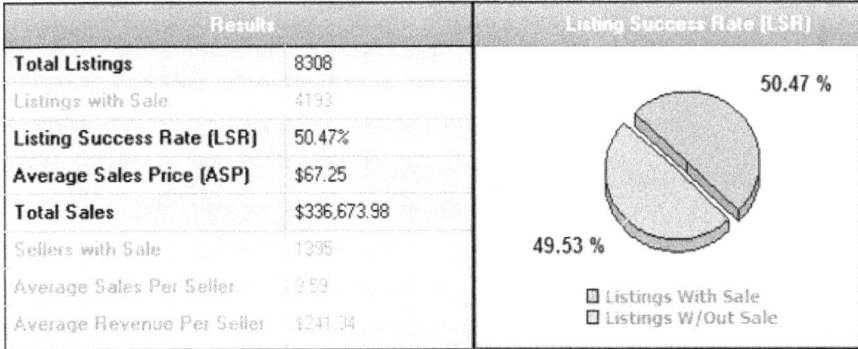

Results		Listing Success Rate (LSR)
Total Listings	8308	
Listings with Sale	4193	
Listing Success Rate (LSR)	50.47%	
Average Sales Price (ASP)	$67.25	
Total Sales	$336,673.98	
Sellers with Sale	1395	
Average Sales Per Seller	3.59	
Average Revenue Per Seller	$241.34	

(c) HammerTap, LLC. Feb. 10 to Feb. 16, 2007.   ····:HammerTap

Figure 5.4: Week 3 Snapshot for Remote-Control Aircraft

Week 4

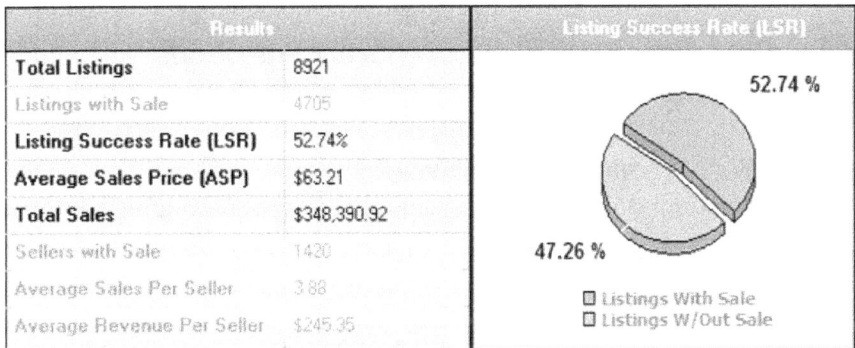

Results		Listing Success Rate (LSR)
Total Listings	8921	
Listings with Sale	4705	
Listing Success Rate (LSR)	52.74%	
Average Sales Price (ASP)	$63.21	
Total Sales	$348,390.92	
Sellers with Sale	1420	
Average Sales Per Seller	3.88	
Average Revenue Per Seller	$245.35	

(c) HammerTap, LLC., Feb. 17 to Feb. 23, 2007.   ····:HammerTap

Figure 5.5: Week 4 Snapshot for Remote-Control Aircraft

Comparing the results over time provides us some subtle clues about how this product has performed over time, and the direction it's going in. Table 5.1, below, pulls it all together.

Week	# Listings	LSR	ASP	Total $
1	9328	46.55%	$63.97	$337,868
2	9218	47.92%	$64.26	$337,798
3	8308	50.47%	$67.25	$336,673
4	8921	52.74%	$63.21	$348,390

Table 5.1: Week-by-Week Demand Comparison

There's a short and long explanation of how this product performed over time.

The short explanation is that it is remarkably stable, with an upturn in the overall dollars consumers are spending for this product on the market.

The long explanation is that this product has not remained static. We do not see a drop in conversion rate (LSR) or selling price (ASP) over the four weeks. On the contrary, we see a climb in overall sales (Total $).

Although the total number of listings (supply) has decreased by five hundred listings from week one to week four (1,000 from week one to week three), we see an increase in Total Sales—an $11,000 difference from week one to week four.

This is encouraging. It doesn't necessarily mean that we will see a sharp increase in sales. But at the same time, we can definitely see that this product is not on its way down. With this information, you could predict that steady sales will continue.

Where is Your Product in Its Life Cycle?

Every product goes through a cycle that begins with a little interest, then attracts more buyers (demand) and not enough sellers (supply), and gradually ends up with too many sellers (supply) and not enough buyers (demand).

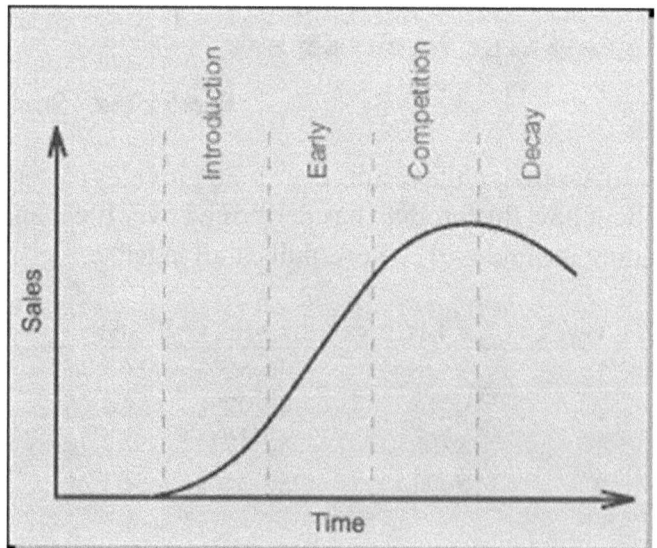

Figure 5.6:
The Product Life Cycle

So how do you decide where a product is in its life cycle? Again, we turn to the data to find out. What we're looking for is how supply and demand change over time. Figure 5.6 gives us quick reference way to remember:

Early Phase: Increasing buyers, few sellers
Competition Phase: Buyers remain steady, but competition is increasing
Decay Phase: Decreasing buyers with even more sellers

Quiz:
From looking at Figure 5.6, which phase in the product life cycle has the greatest sales potential?

Answer:
The Early Phase. You can see the curve in this phase is the sharpest and most steady increase in sales.

Let's take a closer look at each phase, so you'll know it when you see it in the data.

Early Phase

In the Early Phase, interest is just waking up, but there's still not a lot of supply. This means that both supply and demand increase during this phase. But how do you know if you are near the beginning or end of this phase? By looking at the supply and the number of sellers.

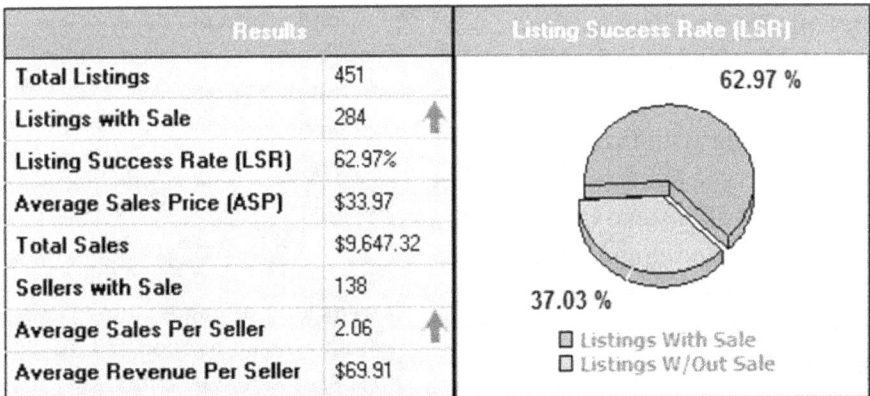

Results		Listing Success Rate (LSR)
Total Listings	451	62.97 %
Listings with Sale	284	
Listing Success Rate (LSR)	62.97%	
Average Sales Price (ASP)	$33.97	
Total Sales	$9,647.32	
Sellers with Sale	138	
Average Sales Per Seller	2.06	37.03 %
Average Revenue Per Seller	$69.91	☐ Listings With Sale ☐ Listings W/Out Sale

(c) HammerTap, Sept. 2006.

····HammerTap

Figure 5.7: Early Phase with Rising LSR and Sales Per Seller

Figure 5.7 shows a product near the beginning of the Early Phase. If this is the case, we can anticipate that both supply and demand will increase, along with the number of sales. This means that demand for the product is rising to match market saturation.

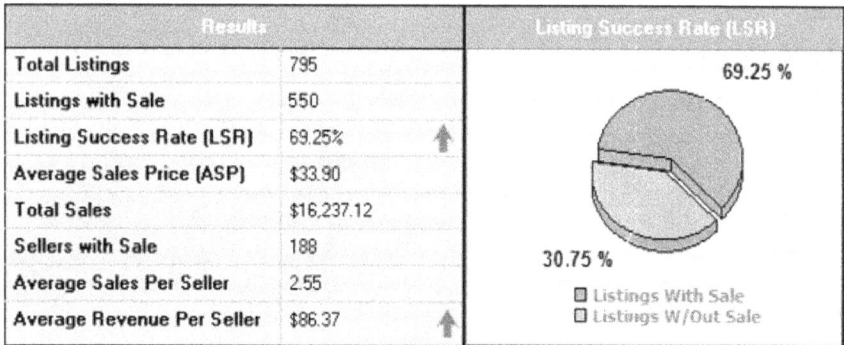

Results		Listing Success Rate (LSR)
Total Listings	795	69.25 %
Listings with Sale	550	
Listing Success Rate (LSR)	69.25%	
Average Sales Price (ASP)	$33.90	
Total Sales	$16,237.12	
Sellers with Sale	188	
Average Sales Per Seller	2.55	30.75 %
Average Revenue Per Seller	$86.37	☐ Listings With Sale ☐ Listings W/Out Sale

(c) HammerTap, Sept., 2006.

····⋮HammerTap

Figure 5.8: Early Phase with Rising LSR and Average Rev Per Seller

Later, we research the same product again to see where the product is now, within the life cycle. Figure 5.8 shows that our anticipations were correct. Our supply has increased from four hundred fifty-one listings to seven hundred ninety-five listings. Our demand has increased, with LSR rising from 62.97% to 69.25%.

But along with this increase, we also have more sellers in the market now, with 188 instead of only 138 when we started. Figure 5.8 also shows that each seller is making a much higher profit than they were before: $16.26 to be exact.

Competition Phase

Because many sellers are making a nice profit with little competition in the Early Phase, other sellers will be drawn to the market.

Although demand is still high, the number of listings (supply) is going to quickly catch up and balance out with demand. As the number of listings increases, the LSR remains steady (this is the balance). Also, the number of sellers is increasing dramatically. These are all indicators that we are well into the Competition Phase.

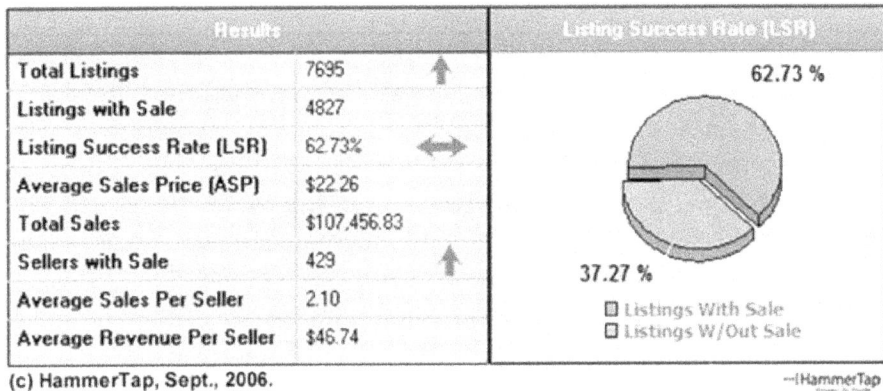

Results		
Total Listings	7695	↑
Listings with Sale	4827	
Listing Success Rate (LSR)	62.73%	↔
Average Sales Price (ASP)	$22.26	
Total Sales	$107,456.83	
Sellers with Sale	429	↑
Average Sales Per Seller	2.10	
Average Revenue Per Seller	$46.74	

Listing Success Rate (LSR)

62.73 %

37.27 %

☐ Listings With Sale
☐ Listings W/Out Sale

(c) HammerTap, Sept., 2006.

—[HammerTap

Figure 5.9: Competition Phase with Rising Competition and Sellers with Sale

Figure 5.9 illustrates the same product much later in time. We can see that the number of listings and the number of sellers has drastically increased. However, sales rates (LSR) have remained steady and the sales price has dropped.

We know we've hit the Competition Phase when supply rises to match demand. There is no shortage, and there seems to be little surplus.

Decay Phase

During the Decay Phase, the market is completely saturated (notice 20,000 listings in Figure 5.10, below). Demand is dropping off (reflected in the LSR), and there is way too much competition for most people to make break-even prices (more than 2,300 sellers). Compare the results in figure 5.10 to those in the Early and Competition Phases.

Results			Listing Success Rate (LSR)
Total Listings	20000	↑	
Listings with Sale	7945		
Listing Success Rate (LSR)	39.73%	↓	
Average Sales Price (ASP)	$15.76		
Total Sales	$125,239.97		
Sellers with Sale	2359	↑	
Average Sales Per Seller	3.37		
Average Revenue Per Seller	$53.09	↓	

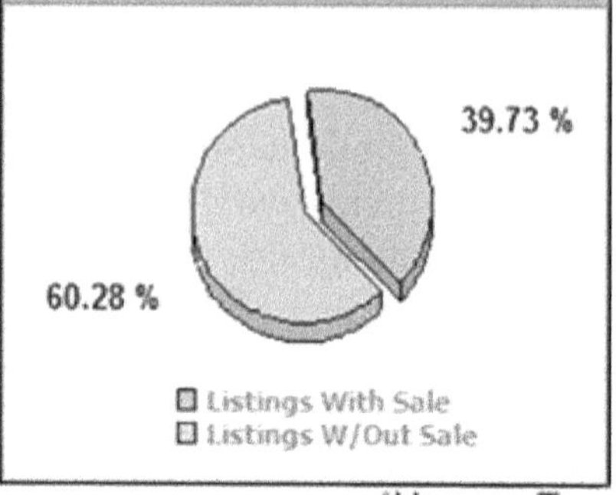

(c) HammerTap, Sept., 2006.   ⋯HammerTap

Figure 5.10: Decay Phase with Maximum Competition and Plummeting LSR

Strategies for Life-Cycle Phases

Now that you know all about the product life cycle, it's time to get excited. Why? Because I'm not going to recommend just one or two of the phases to operate your business in. You can sell a product, **for a profit,** during any phase of its life cycle if you have:

- the strategies
- the sources

It all depends on the right circumstances. And you're the one who creates the right circumstances. On the next page are your strategies in a nutshell.

Look carefully at the following strategies. Do you see how different the approaches are, depending on the life-cycle phase the product is in? I hope you are beginning to see why it's so important to understand where your product is in its life cycle.

The key in all of this is to understand that not just your selling strategies will change, based on your knowledge of the product's life cycle. Your sourcing strategies will change, too.

Fad vs. Fashion

Here's where following the rules of the product life cycle gets a little tricky. Essentially, there are two types of products: fads and fashions. Fads move quickly through their life cycles and then die, never to return.

Phase	Demand	Supply	Selling Strategies
Early Phase	High	Low	Product is very expensive early on in the product cycle, but if your sources can get you a sellable product with a window of opportunity before it is available to the general marketplace, you can expect to make some of the highest profits on eBay during this stage. Demand is very high and supply is low.
Competition	Leveling	Increasing	Selling here is where most traditional businesses compete. Higher margins come from efficiency, good supply relationships, and volume discounts. However, sellers must constantly be aware of the upcoming shift to the end of the product life cycle.
Decay Phase	Low	High	Selling here is tricky, risky, and timing-intensive. The goal is to buy product in volume just as it hits liquidation channels but before demand has dried up as the result of market saturation or the public's anticipation of the replacement product. There is usually a window here where sellers can make a small profit by buying at liquidation prices and selling at near-retail prices, but this is usually a very small window.

Table 5.2: Selling Strategies for Life Cycle Phases

Can't think of a fad? Here are a few reminders: pet rocks, PogsTM, FurbiesTM, Beanie BabiesTM, Razor® scooters, mood rings, TrollTM dolls, Girbaud® jeans. Fads. All of them.

Fashions move through their life cycles more slowly, and then might repeat them over and over. Here are some examples of fashions: sporting equipment, jewelry, cell phones, mp3 players, purses and handbags, cameras and camcorders, holiday décor. You get my point.

While fads never seem to make it back, fashion usually comes back, although it may not be the same exact model that repeats over and over.

Let's take golf clubs, for example. Golf club manufacturers will sell clubs year after year. But, whenever they make a new model, the old one phases out of the market and the new one takes its place. Savvy sellers will watch for this cycle to repeat and plan accordingly.

Seasonal Life Cycles

If there is one thing that can drastically affect your sales and profits in a short amount of time, it's seasonal and holiday trends. Around every change in season, or around every holiday, you will see a change in the product life cycle.

For example, I had a friend who was selling chocolates during Valentine's Day. She wanted to know when to start selling chocolates and when to stop selling them.

She looked back at last year's data and found out exactly when to begin selling chocolate. She wasn't too surprised at the timing for when to start offering her seasonal items. But, she was shocked that sales didn't simmer down until after the weekend after Valentines. Sellers who were still selling during those few days after Valentines could make a killing—because everyone else had already dropped out!

"When is My Product Going to Be in Season?"

To answer this question, you will need to study last year's listings in your market research tool. Looking at a snapshot of what took place in the market last year at this time can help us understand when our product will be in or out of season. Once you do this, you'll want to narrow your time frame to study your product week-by-week.

Once you've done the research, what are you looking for? You are watching for indicators in last year's research that show you that the product is entering the Competition Phase (as explained earlier in this chapter).

These results also help with items that sell all year, but which are replaced by newer models, such as software items or gaming consoles.

When are Sales for My Seasonal Item Going to Decline?

The answer to this question is nearly identical to the last one. Except this time you are watching for Decay-Phase indicators (as covered earlier in this chapter). This information should show you when to begin easing out of the market.

Grow My Profits Study Example

Study participant Tim Reynolds mastered the principles of the product life cycle early on in our study and found it to be very profitable. Read an excerpt from his business journal below:

"The use of HammerTap is becoming profitable for me. I have been going through my current products, and I am finding out where the product is in their life cycle. From the research on product life cycle, I have found that I have made some poor choices, or better, poor timing, on when I have made some of my purchases. I no longer just purchase a product just because it is hot."

This was a break-through for Tim, and for the other study participants, too. What he learned during the study is what I hope you will learn, also. He learned to give up his prejudices and personal "hunches" about how a product would perform, and began looking to the research to find answers based on solid evidence.

Looking to the research for answers doesn't mean blind acceptance. It includes trying to punch holes in the answers you think you're getting. But, if the research stands up to your poking and prodding, it's time to go with it!

Highlights:
- Tim profited from his knowledge of the product life-cycle.
- He also learned to put aside his hunches for answers based on evidence (research).

How Much Can I Afford to Pay?

CHAPTER 6

You've found a product that sells 99.99% of the time! Your chances of not selling are one in a 1,000. And it seems that there is an unlimited amount of room on the market for more of the product. You'd be crazy not to go for it, right?

You approach a vendor and share the incredible news. Nine hundred ninety-nine out of every 1,000 listings with that product sell on the eBay market. Everyone is happy. You've hit the jackpot and you start making plans to take the whole family to Disneyland to celebrate.

But something isn't right with this picture.

In this chapter, Jen talks about:

- 100% of nothing is still nothing
- Foundation for the cost calculation
- Understanding your hard costs
- Maximum cost formula

100% of Nothing is Still Nothing

I don't want to be a party pooper. I'm just the messenger. Let's say that your research shows that your product sells for around $112, on average. When you look for a product source, you find that your product costs $113. I know you wouldn't really pay a dollar more for a product than you could sell it for—even if you can sell it 99.99% of

Cowie & Cano 47

the time—but humor me for a minute. Even 100% of nothing is still nothing.

Here's another scenario. What if you can get the item for $105. Is it worth it then? Maybe and maybe not. Perhaps when you add your selling fees to the cost of the item, you'll still end up losing money.

Do you see what I'm getting at here? Your goal is to make money. If you remember, we discussed figuring out what's hot for you during Chapter 3. Your cost to source the product is part of what makes a product hot for you.

In a later chapter, Robin is going to talk about how to approach your distributor and how to build that relationship. But I have one point to make about your initial contact. Think about how much smoother it will go, how much more confidence you'll have, if you know the highest amount you can pay for the item and still make a profit.

After you read this chapter, you'll never again be surprised about how much or how little profit you actually bring in when you make your first sales with the item. You will know that answer before you begin.

Foundation for the Cost Calculation

Our cost calculations can't be based on "fuzzy" data. For the formulas to work, we want solid information about specific products. There is no rounding or guesstimating. For setting profit-making goals, every penny counts.

In Chapter 3, we talked about using research to find hot products. I used that method to find quivers that sell well in the Quivers in the Archery > Bows and Shooting Accessories category and came up with the following candidates:

Product	LSR	ASP	Number of Listings
Trophy Ridge Hunter	94.64%	$47.62	56
Hoyt Duralite	100%	$43.30	8
Bear	79.46%	$35.85	112

Table 6.1: LSRs and ASPs for Three Specific Quivers (Jan. 27 – Feb. 26, 2007)

To decide how much you can afford to pay for your product, you first need to know how much it sells for and how often it sells. The table above gives this information for three products.

The information in Table 6.1 is the foundation I'll use to calculate the amount I can afford to pay for a product.

Analysis Tip: Gather Enough Information

Notice that Hoyt Duralite quivers had an ASP of 100%. This means that every listing sold. But, look a little closer. There were only eight listings in all. Eight listings are probably not enough to base a solid selling decision on. True, they might be showing us a new, emerging product. But the 100% sell-through rate might just be a fluke, also.

Have some caution when basing selling and buying decisions on too little data.

Understanding Your Hard Costs

In addition to knowing how much you can sell the item for, and how often you'll sell it, you need a detailed understanding of your hard costs. What do I mean by hard costs? Some of them are insertion fees, payment/merchant fees, shipping and handling costs, final value fees, and your time.

Let's review each cost, and some of the considerations for each of them. For the sake of the break-even formula I'll show you later, I'm going to divide your costs into three categories:

• Insertion Fees
• Costs of Doing Business (CODB)
• Your Time

Insertion Fees

For the formula I'll share with you in just a few pages, you need to have your insertion fees separate from your other fees. (Don't ask me why. It's part of the "magic" formula one of HammerTap's numerical geniuses created just for this purpose.)

Your insertion fees include the base cost to list the item, plus any listing upgrade fees (on items such as gallery picture, highlight, and bold).

Of course, you already know you can get a fairly exact value for your insertion fees, ahead of time, in a few ways. Let me just remind you:

- http://pages.ebay.com/help/sell/fees.html
- eBay fee calculators, such as http://pages.ebay.com/help/sell/fees.html. (shows PayPal and eBay fees) and HammerTap's FeeFinder (shows payment, eBay, and shipping fees)

For the Trophy Ridge Hunter, my research shows that the best starting price is going to be around $9.99. My research also shows that selling with a Gallery picture will help me sell more listings at a higher price. So, I'm definitely going to do that. (Check out Chapter 12 for more details about optimizing your listings.)

- Basic Insertion fee: $.40
- Gallery Picture: $.35
- **Total Insertion Fee: $.75**

Cost of Doing Business

You've probably already found business costs lurking in every corner. Time to bring them all out into the open and take a good look at them. Think about every penny you spend in order to get that product to the customer's door, and plan accordingly.

- payment/merchant fees
- shipping and handling costs
- final value fees

Here are some scenarios to think about:
- **Merchant Account:** Your merchant account probably costs you about 2.2% plus $.30 per transaction. On an item you'll sell for $20, that's $.75. Don't forget to add that to your cost of doing business.
- **Dropship Fees:** Your distributor may charge a drop ship fee per item.
- **Mailing Supplies:** Maybe you will buy boxes and labels for shipping wholesale products you bought in bulk.
- **Receiving Bulk Shipments:** You might buy products in bulk, and then ship them yourself. When you buy a few cases of

products from a light bulk wholesaler, for example, it's going to cost you a certain amount of money to have those cases shipped to you. If you buy a bulk load of two hundred products, and you pay $50 in shipping to get that bulk load delivered to you, you need to remember to add $.25 to your cost of doing business for each of those two hundred products!

This process may seem complicated, but it's really not. Just take the figures one at a time, and you'll arrive at your cost of doing business. Take a look at an example of my costs of doing business for the Trophy Ridge Hunter quiver:

Drop Ship Fee = $1.50
PayPal = $1.63
Final Value Fee = $1.99
Cost of Doing Business = $5.12

Your Time

With all of your costs of doing business, don't forget to pay yourself!

It's tough, but you have to decide how much your time is worth, at a minimum. No one knows better than an eBay seller that selling can be time-consuming. And if you're only making enough to pay everyone else, you're just spinning your wheels.

It takes time to create your listing. Then, you have to package and ship the item. There might be several other steps between your initial listing efforts to the delivery of the product. And your time is valuable. What we want to do during this step is determine how much your time is worth, at a minimum.

Let's look at the Trophy Ridge Hunter example. If it takes me an average of ten minutes per listing (if I plan to list the same product over and over), then I know I can fulfill on six listings per hour, from start to finish.

On the next page is the formula:

Maximum Cost Formula

Before we move on to the break-even formula, let's review some information about selling the Trophy Ridge Hunter quiver:

LSR: 94.64%
ASP: $47.62
Insertion Fees: $.75
Cost of Doing Business: $5.12
My Time: $5

And now, the moment you've been waiting for. Below is the formula for calculating how much you can afford to pay for your product.

Maximum Cost Formula

$$\text{Maximum Cost} = \text{ASP} - \left[\left(\frac{\text{Insertion Fees}}{\text{LSR}}\right) + \text{CODB} + \text{Time Value}\right]$$

Example:

$$\$47.62 - \left[\left(\frac{\$.75}{94.64\%}\right) + \$5.12 + 5\right] = \$36.71$$

Before we leave this formula, let's just take a moment to talk about the order that you do the math in:

1. First, divide the insertion fee by the LSR (listing success rate).
2. Next, add your CODB (cost of doing business) and your time value (what your time is worth, per listing, in dollars).

3. Then, subtract that number from your ASP (average selling price).

Now, before you approach your product source representative, you will have a key bargaining chip—that is the knowledge of how much you can afford to pay for your product.

Grow My Profits Study Example

Once you have identified your costs and profit goals like we did in this chapter, you can look for other ways to cut your costs aside from finding the best prices for your products from a wholesaler.

Bryan Mills, a Grow My Profits study participant, was able to identify his costs of doing business (CODB) and use different strategies for lowering those costs. Below is an excerpt from his business journal.

"This week my cost-cutting measures allowed me to make about the same amount of profit with less work and expenditures. Now all I need to do is increase my sales in order to make a decent amount of money on eBay. My goals are becoming so much more clear each time I do this exercise."

By the end of the study, Bryan had mastered this concept. He used his research to figure out how to cut costs he didn't even know weren't necessary in order to make products profitable for him.

Highlights:
- Through research, Bryan discovered unnecessary costs.
- Cost-cutting strategies made products more affordable for Bryan.

7

Evaluating Risks

Jen and I were talking about risk and I related this story to her:

I was the producer of the *Blair Witch Project*. I first became involved in it early 1997. The directors and the other producer had been trying to make it for a year. I had had some success in my other businesses and thought Blair was the best idea I had ever heard for an independent movie.

So I put in the first monies to help the Blair Witch Project get made. I then set about raising the remaining funds. Contrary to popular belief, Blair Witch DID NOT cost $30,000. It cost a lot more than that, and for first-time filmmakers, it was difficult to get investors to take a risk on us. I did two things to get investors to join me in my venture:

1. I researched other low-budget horror films and documented their budgets and the returns they had made. It became pretty clear that a movie at our budget level that was halfway decent could easily make back our budget.
2. Our film was accepted by the famous Sundance Film Festival and finally investors started to drop their doubts—and their dollars. It took research and timing to finally get all the money raised.

When it comes to research, you should have two main priorities: increase profit and reduce risk.

You have new competitors every day. Consumer tastes, demand, and habits change all the time. We've spent the last several chapters talking about how to anticipate these changes.

In this chapter, Jen teaches you how to:

- Identify potential risk
- Decide whether a risk is acceptable or unacceptable
- Reduce risk with market research

Let's shift perspective from using research to anticipate what sells to using research to anticipate risk. How are you going evaluate, reduce, and eliminate risk in your business?

First, you can't expect to base your sales solely on guesswork—that's risk in itself. Remember my friend who bought a shipment of women's clothing she couldn't sell? We've already addressed how you can eliminate much of that risk through research. By now you have a solid foundation on which to base more sound and informed decisions about product sourcing.

However—and this is my second fact about risk—every profitable business has some risk involved. If it didn't everyone would be in business. We'd all be wildly successful and rolling in money. What's more, if doing business didn't involve risk, you would only have to work hard to make great money—and we all know, unfortunately, that's not always the case. So what's the trick?

In order to be successful, you need to effectively eliminate and accept risk. Using research can help you accomplish both.

Identifying Potential Risk

If you're like me, you probably started your eBay adventure selling odds and ends around the house. I quickly found how profitable and easy selling online really is. But all good things must come to an end, and that's exactly what happened with my odds and ends.

But now that you're hooked, you need to find some products to sell. As you're looking, you're quickly finding out that a small investment of time and money is now required. No need to panic! It's not the end of the world. We just need to sit down and think of all the risks you will face as you invest in products to sell.

Here is a short list to help you get started:

1. **What if my profit margins are too small?** You've found a hot product that has a high success rate, but you're not making the money you expected.
2. **What if I don't make money on it at all?** It's selling like hotcakes but you're losing money on every sale. Instead of making money online you are now losing money.
3. **What if the product won't sell?** No one wants to be stuck with $1,000 (or any amount) in inventory that isn't moving.
4. **If it doesn't sell, I'll still have eBay fees to pay.** If you list and don't sell, you still have the cost of doing business to worry about.
5. **What if I have inventory left over that I can't move?** This is closely related to the product not selling at all. Who can afford unsold inventory that won't sell?
6. **What if there is too much competition?** With sellers constantly entering the market, your prices may be undercut or your products may be less enticing.
7. **What if there is a drastic change in the market?** You just bought a hundred video games to find out that they are in the Decay Phase of their product life cycle.
8. **What if my drop shipper is not reliable?** You've sold a dozen products, but none of them have been shipped.

Once you have your own risks jotted down, hide them under your pillow for the Risk Fairy to come and sweep them away. Problem solved!

You might laugh at my suggestion, but if you're not taking an honest look at your risks and deciding what to do about them, the outcome will be the same. So let's address risks the logical way, and in our case, the statistical way.

Deciding Which Risks are Acceptable

Throughout all previous chapters we have used research to make more informed decisions concerning product sourcing. In other words, we have used research to reduce risk. But why not just eliminate risk altogether?

Unfortunately, there will always be some risk involved in business. But that's also fortunate for you because it keeps the competition down. Risk is what stops too many sellers from competing for their slice of the pie.

But you want your slice of the pie! Why give it to someone else when you could have it? In order to have it, you need to understand the risks involved in getting it. However, some risks are acceptable, while others are not.

How do you determine if a risk is acceptable or unacceptable? **Acceptable risks are risks you are willing to take that have a way out** (or a Plan B). These are the risks we can live with, the risks we accept as a normal part of our business.

Unacceptable risks, though, leave no room for a way out or a Plan B. With unacceptable risks, you end up feeling like you've backed yourself into a corner with no way out. Obviously we want to eliminate unacceptable risks—meaning we are not willing to accept them because there is no backup plan.

Analysis Tip: Acceptable vs. Unacceptable Risks
Acceptable risks have a backup plan. Unacceptable risks have no way out or no way to soften the consequences.

For example, an acceptable risk may be small profit margins. You can accept the risk of your profit margins being too small because you can find ways to increase your margins, or liquidate your inventory and break even. The risk becomes acceptable because you can develop a Plan B.

An example of an unacceptable risk might be an unreliable drop shipper that can lead to unhappy customers. Unhappy customers lead to negative feedback, lost income on return sales, and lost income on future sales because of a bad track record. This risk is unacceptable because you cannot develop a Plan B. A bunch of negative feedback has no backup plan to fix the problem.

Do you see the difference between these two types of risks?

When should you determine if a risk regarding a specific product is acceptable or unacceptable?

Answer:

Before you purchase the product. Remember that you don't want to back yourself into a corner. You need a way out. Developing a Plan B is part of accepting the risk involved. If there is no Plan B, and you accept the risk, it's important to fully understand the potential consequences in the long run.

Using Research to Reduce Potential Risk

Once you have accepted the risks you can afford to take, the key is to then reduce the risk as much as possible. You need to find a solution to the "what ifs" we have addressed so you don't back yourself into a corner.

Remember my friend who bought all those jeans because of what she discovered on a hot list? She didn't think about what she would do if the product didn't sell.

Of course you have used research in all the previous chapters to reduce much of the risk involved in investing in a product to sell. You've learned how to really identify hot products, to determine your market potential, and to find the break-even price you can pay for your products. Already you can greatly reduce the risk, but now you need a backup plan, a Plan B, for the risks you're willing to take on.

Let's look at one of the risks we have identified.

"What if my profit margins are too small?"

No doubt this question has crossed your mind. What if you get a hot-selling product, but you profit margins are so small that you are making less than minimum wage for the time you are putting into it? Is there anything you can do to increase your margins?

This question should lead you right to your Plan B. And you should develop the plan before you even invest in the products. The greatest advantage of research is that it is going to tell you whether your Plan B is going to work *in advance*.

Get creative and look for specific solutions to specific problems.

Using Research to Develop Plan B

As an eBay seller, you face new obstacles, challenges, and risks on a regular basis. I'd like to show you several ways to use research to come up with your Plan B.

Narrow profit margins is a fairly common risk on the eBay marketplace. So, we'll use that as our example in the following strategies.

Bundle Complementary Products
Strategy: Increase Selling Price Per Item

Let's say you want to sell a Nintendo® Wii™ gaming console, but your initial research shows that the margin is too narrow. You wonder if you might be able to sell at a higher profit margin if you include some games and controllers with the console.

You turn to research to decide.

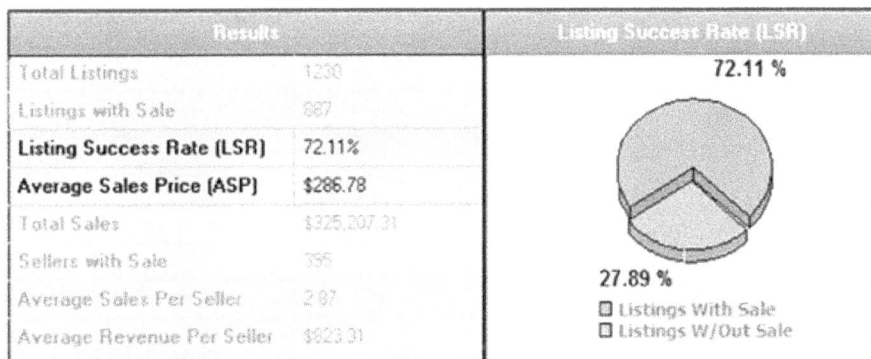

Results		Listing Success Rate (LSR)
Total Listings	1230	72.11 %
Listings with Sale	887	
Listing Success Rate (LSR)	72.11%	
Average Sales Price (ASP)	$286.78	
Total Sales	$325,207.31	
Sellers with Sale	395	
Average Sales Per Seller	2.87	27.89 %
Average Revenue Per Seller	$823.31	☐ Listings With Sale ☐ Listings W/Out Sale

(c)Hammertap, Feb. 6 - Mar. 7, 2007. Category #1249   ┄┄HammerTap

Figure 7.1: Nintendo Wii Gaming Consoles Sold Alone

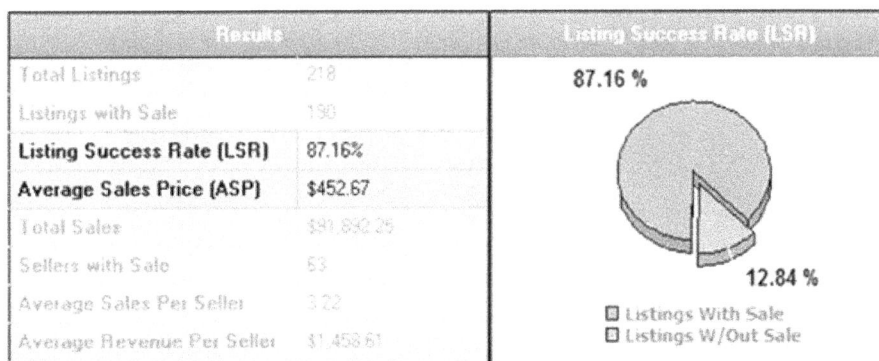

Results		Listing Success Rate (LSR)
Total Listings	218	87.16 %
Listings with Sale	190	
Listing Success Rate (LSR)	87.16%	
Average Sales Price (ASP)	$452.67	
Total Sales	$91,890.25	
Sellers with Sale	53	
Average Sales Per Seller	3.22	12.84 %
Average Revenue Per Seller	$1,458.61	☐ Listings With Sale ☐ Listings W/Out Sale

(c) HammerTap, Feb. 7 - Mar. 7, 2007. Category # 1249   ┄┄HammerTap

Figure 7.2: Nintendo Wii Consoles with Controllers and Games

After finding this information, you would then calculate how much your costs would be if you bundled controllers, games, and the console in your listings. This will help you figure out whether your Plan B will increase your margins.

Separate Complementary Products
Strategy: Increase Selling Price Per Item

Now let's say you want to sell the TV series FriendsTM. But, the selling margin on the series is too narrow. You wonder if you might be able to make more money if you sell each DVD in the series separately, rather than as a set.

Again, you turn to research to decide.

Results		Listing Success Rate (LSR)
Total Listings	888	
Listings with Sale	516	
Listing Success Rate (LSR)	75.00%	
Average Sales Price (ASP)	$134.46	
Total Sales	$89,243.03	
Sellers with Sale	163	
Average Sales Per Seller	4.03	
Average Revenue Per Seller	$541.98	

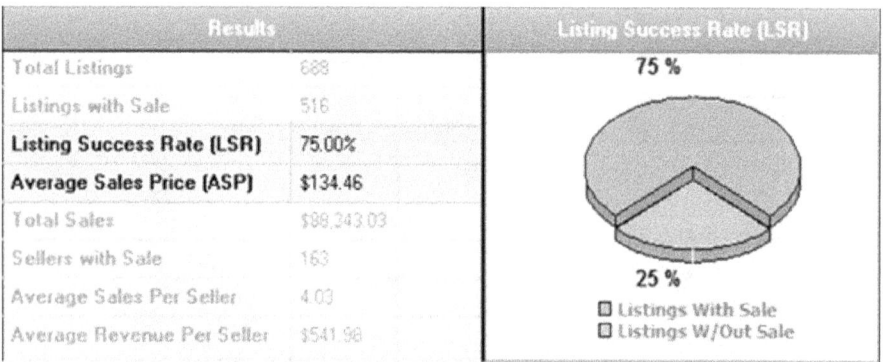

(c)HammerTap, Feb 7 - Mar 7, 2007. Category #617   ····:HammerTap

Figure 7.3: Friends, the Complete Series

Results		Listing Success Rate (LSR)
Total Listings	30	
Listings with Sale	27	
Listing Success Rate (LSR)	90.00%	
Average Sales Price (ASP)	$16.82	
Total Sales	$521.55	
Sellers with Sale	14	
Average Sales Per Seller	2.21	
Average Revenue Per Seller	$37.25	

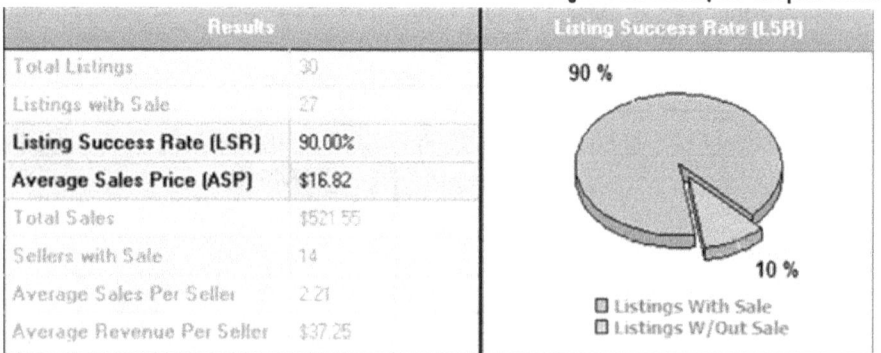

(c)HammerTap, Feb. 7 - Mar. 7, 2007. Category #617   ····:HammerTap

Figure 7.4: Friends, Season Eight

From our initial research, it looks like season eight will give us a better conversion rate, and a better profit margin than if we sell the complete series.

Combine Shipping or Give a Break in Shipping
Strategy: Create Buying Urgency to Increase Selling Price
Once again, you've found a product with low profit margins. Try out how a break in shipping affects other products you sell that are similar. Look to see how much other sellers are charging for shipping. You might be able to charge a little less and stimulate higher ending prices on your listings.

Reduce Your Time Per Listing
Strategy: Decrease Listing Costs
Look for areas where you can cut back on time. If you reduce the time it takes to fulfill on a product from ten minutes to six minutes, you now have the potential to sell 40% more per hour, and increase your profits by 40% per hour.

Sell a Higher Volume Per Listing
Strategy: Decrease Listing Costs
Let's say you're selling disposable cameras, which do not have an impressive success rate. See Figure 7.5

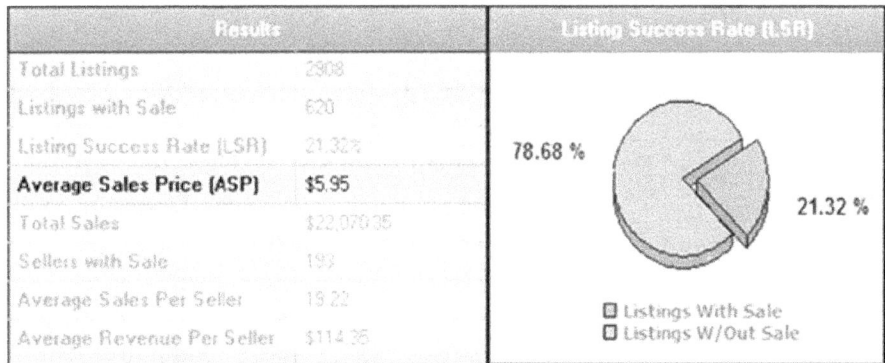

Results		Listing Success Rate (LSR)
Total Listings	2908	
Listings with Sale	620	78.68 %
Listing Success Rate (LSR)	21.32%	
Average Sales Price (ASP)	**$5.95**	21.32 %
Total Sales	$22,070.95	
Sellers with Sale	193	
Average Sales Per Seller	19.22	☐ Listings With Sale
Average Revenue Per Seller	$114.35	☐ Listings W/Out Sale

(c) HammerTap, March, 2007.   ⋯HammerTap

Figure 7.5: Success Rate and Selling Price for Disposable Cameras*
* (Research done for category 73449, Cameras and Photo> Film Cameras> Disposable.
Performed on March 9, 2007.)

As you can see, my profit margins will be pretty low because I am spending a lot of money on my listing fees. But how can I reduce my fees and increase my profit margins?

I researched the ASP of camera bundles to find out how I might decrease my selling costs. If I decrease the number of listings, I also decrease my listing fees. Table 7.1 shows my results.

Camera Type	Lot Size	Price	Price Per Camera
Kodak™ Funsaver	7	$20.50	$2.93
	4	$10.70	$2.68
	3	$6.50	$2.17
Water & Sport	4	$32.00	$8.00
	3	$14.99	$5.00
	1	$5.00	$5.00
Powerflash™	10	$23.00	$2.30
	5	$6.99	$1.40
	4	$9.99	$2.50
	3	$9.75	$3.75
	2	$0.99	$0.50

Table 7.1 – Comparison of Selling Cameras by the Bundle

We've done it! We have developed a Plan B. And this is just one of the ways to do it. Every Plan B for any specific risk can have multiple strategies. The important thing to practice is developing the strategies before you invest in a product. If you cannot develop backup plans, the risks may be too high for your product.

During the Grow My Profits study, one of our participants used this strategy to increase his profit margins. Following is his account.

Grow My Profits Study Example

At the beginning of the study, Bryan Mills was selling his items one at a time, at a 27% success rate. Try as he might, he was still not making the kind of profit he wanted to. When he went deeper into the research for selling strategies, he found that if he bundled his products, selling five at a time, his success rate increased and he sold more items over time:

Week 1:
Total Auctions Ended = 107
Total number sold = 29
% Successful Auctions = 27.10%

Week 8:
Total Auctions Ended = 32
Total number sold = 38 (remember, Bryan was selling more than one item/listing)
% Successful Auctions = 42%

As you can see from the numbers above, the risk in the beginning was that Bryan was really spinning his wheels. He was wasting a lot of time on activities that didn't make a lot of money, and he was spending more on listing fees than he needed to.

By the end of the study, he was making more revenue with only 32 listings than he was with 107. During week 1 he sold 29 items with 107 listings. But during week 8, he sold 38 with just 32 listings (remember, each listing included multiple items this time). How did this impact his profit? Think back to our profit formulas in Chapter 6. He took into account, and reduced:

- Listing fees
- Time it takes to list

Through his new strategy, Bryan had lowered the risks associated with selling this particular item. His Plan B was to look at ways he could either cut costs to run the listings or to increase the price he got. He soon found that he couldn't make more money per listing if he continued listing single items. So he turned to cutting costs to list.

In this case, he was able to cut down on costs for both fees and time. Cutting his costs increased his margins for those items.

Are there items you are selling right now that you could use a similar strategy for?

Highlights:

- Bryan's Plan B to reduce risk included cutting costs and decreasing the time he spent on each listing.
- Through research, Bryan discovered how to make more sales with fewer listings.

Section 3

Source—Where to Get It

"The Internet will help achieve 'friction free capitalism' by putting buyer and seller in direct contact and providing more information to both about each other."

– Bill Gates, Bill Gates A&E Biography

How Do I Find a Vendor for My Product?

8

I've been the co-host of The Entrepreneur Magazine Product Sourcing Radio Show for two years now, and I'm also the contributing editor on Product Sourcing for eBay Radio. The two questions most frequently asked on BOTH these shows are:

1. What should I sell on eBay?
2. Where can I find a reliable supplier?

Jen has made a good start to answering "What should I sell?" Now, I'm going to build on that and tackle question two while constantly referring back to question one. Remember our analogy of the juggler? It is important to realize that researching, sourcing, and selling are not only interrelated processes, but tasks that you do simultaneously. That means you should continuously be researching, sourcing, and selling at the same time.

My company, Worldwide Brands, has been dedicated to answering these two questions for seven years; and, consequently, we have examined every possible answer in some great detail. In this chapter, we're going to attack the top three methods of finding a vendor for your product. Along the way, I will highlight some common product sourcing mistakes that retailers make. These top three methods are used by every successful online seller I know.

In this chapter, Robin talks about the top three methods for finding suppliers:

1. Going to the source (a method of finding suppliers through manufacturers)
2. Tradeshows, events, journals and associations
3. Reliable Directories – that use the above two methods

What Went Wrong?

Eight years ago, Chris Malta, my partner at Worldwide Brands, was a highly successful systems analyst for KodakR in Rochester, New York. He had risen to the top of the Kodak IT world very rapidly, considering that five years before, Chris was the 6 ft.-8 in. leader of a motley biker gang! At twenty-seven, he decided that he needed to reinvent himself, and he went to college and studied this cool thing called computers. He was so successful at Kodak that it didn't take long for head hunters to come calling.

One made a particularly appealing offer for him to relocate to Orlando, Florida. He bought a house, and moved his entire family down, only to discover that he had been scammed. There was no job. The headhunter had taken the commission and split. Suddenly Chris was faced with another opportunity to reinvent himself!

Sourcing Tip: Smaller Manufacturers are Risky

The manufacturers that sell directly to retailers usually have to do their own distribution because they are typically too small to attract the attention of the large wholesale supply companies. They are generally very small companies that produce limited numbers of specialty items. Buying directly from these small manufacturers can have its pitfalls. Small companies can rarely keep up with a fast-paced sales season, like the annual holiday season. They take longer to produce products and are more likely to run out of stock or go out of business suddenly.

That's when he decided to tackle the world of eCommerce. He had done quite a bit of eCommerce for Kodak and realized that he was in the early days of Yahoo! stores and eBay. He believed that the future of business lay online.

So he opened up shop and—like most of you who are reading this right now—the first thing he did was look for a product to sell. Unfortunately, the experience was a nightmare. He was scammed by a store in a box company who said they had thousands of products pre-loaded and ready to sell. All Chris had to do was purchase the store and run it. He quickly discovered that this company was not the only shark in the product sourcing waters. In fact, Chris ran into so many scams that he decided to set out and find his own suppliers his own way.

Over the years, Worldwide Brands has continued to ferret out product sourcing scams, and we have compiled a useful Product Sourcing Scam report that is in the back of this book as Appendix B. By simply reviewing this list of scammers, you will save thousands of dollars and potential heart aches. Unfortunately, the simple truth is that there are many people online who will simply take advantage of you.

Chris went on to solve his own sourcing problems and created Worldwide Brands. So here is how we and Chris set out finding products to sell.

1. Going to the Source

One of the best ways to locate quality wholesalers is to go directly to the manufacturers.

Manufacturers make products. Authorized wholesalers distribute the products to retailers like yourself. As such, the manufacturer of any product will have a contact list (of their authorized wholesalers) and will be more than happy to share it with you as a retailer. By going to the source (the manufacturer), you'll be able to find out exactly who the legitimate wholesalers are, and then be able to set up wholesale accounts and begin selling their products.

Once in a while, you may find a manufacturer who is willing to sell to you directly, and that's great, but you need to be careful. It's great to deal directly with a manufacturer, but be careful if they are a small company. Larger wholesale suppliers are much more stable and reliable.

Who is the Manufacturer?

Finding the manufacturer of a product is not always as easy as it sounds. You can't just assume you know who the maker is, even if it's a popular brand name. RCA, for example, is manufactured by Thompson Consumer Electronics. You wouldn't know that without looking at the owner's manual for the product, or the serial number sticker on the back. You need to go ALL the way to the top of the manufacturing chain, not just to some subsidiary brand name.

If you have a hard time figuring out who the manufacturer of a product is, your best bet is to simply BUY one of the products you want to sell, or take a notepad to your local mall and inspect a demo product on the store shelf. Take a look at the box, the owner's manual, or any warranty papers that come with it. Check out the model and serial number stickers on the back of the product. Somewhere, you will find the name of the product's manufacturer. Also take a look at the product website, which will often be linked to the manufacturer's website.

Sourcing Tip: Finding the Manufacturer

Many products will use a UPC code (Universal Product Code). Wikipedia.com has a great definition and a number of resources you can use to track the UPC barcode number back to the manufacturer of the product. If you can't find the manufacturer any other way, this is a good technique to use.

Contacting the Manufacturer

Once you have located the manufacturer and their contact number, call or e-mail them, identify yourself using a legal business name (see Getting Legal in the product sourcing tip below), and ask for the sales department. Tell them your company is interested in retailing their products, and you need to speak with a sales representative.

They're going to tell you that they are a manufacturer, and don't sell directly to retailers. Tell them that you understand that; you're just looking for a recommendation for a wholesaler of their products.

It may take some time to get through to a sales rep, and you may have to leave a message. If you don't hear from them within a couple of days, call again. Keep calling back until you speak to someone personally.

When you do get through to a manufacturer's sales rep, you can ask if they will wholesale products to you direct from the factory. But the answer 99.9% of the time is "No, of course not." That's OK. Tell

Sourcing Tip: Getting Legal

Please remember the following two statements:

- Successful wholesale product sourcing means working only with REAL wholesale suppliers.
- You cannot buy from a REAL wholesale supplier if you are not a LEGAL business.

This is the single-most common point of failure for any online business, on eBay or anywhere else. Too many people refuse to take a few simple steps to form a legal business, so that they can work with REAL wholesale suppliers. Getting legal is VERY important, and NOT that hard. Here are the basics (in the U.S.):

1. File your business name.

You need an official business name that's recognized by your state government. You can do this one of two ways:

   A. You can file a corporation with your state. All states in the U.S. have web sites where you can get information on this, and in many cases actually file your business papers online. In most states you can form a corporation easily for less than $100.

   B. A Fictitious Name is a simpler way to register your business when you first start out. This doesn't cost as much as a corporation. In some states, this is called a DBA (Doing Business As), and is obtained from your local county office building for a minimal fee. ($35 would be an average).

If you're not sure which way you want to go, ask an attorney or accountant.

2. Get a "sales tax ID."

In almost every state in the U.S., you are required to have a Tax ID if you're selling products. Some call it a Sales and Use Tax Certificate, some call it a Seller's Permit, etc. It's the same thing. It allows you to collect sales tax on sales you make within your own state. Real wholesale suppliers can not do business with you if you don't have one. In Florida, we can get a tax ID in about 15 minutes for $5, as long as we've formed a legal business.

the sales rep that you would appreciate a list of wholesale suppliers that he or she recommends.

The manufacturer's sales rep has that information, and should not have a problem emailing it to you. Then, start calling those wholesalers.

2. Tradeshows, Events, Journals and Associations

Online retail is big business—Forrester Research estimates that by 2010, 13% of all retail transactions will occur online. That's a significant rise from only 3% in 1999. Maybe that's why it's becoming easier to find things to sell online—more and more wholesalers and manufacturers are willing to work with Internet retailers. Not all, but many are seeing great potential in using web stores as a product outlet.

Product sourcing, however, has been around a lot longer than the Internet. Since the early days of the mercantile system, trade associations and guilds have stepped into the role of providing business-to-business marketplaces, creating a place for the exchange of goods between manufacturers, wholesalers, and retailers. It is the primary method of product sourcing used by ALL retailers. Unfortunately, it is more challenging for small home-based entrepreneurs to gain access to these trading areas.

Here are some of the ways you should be using this well-established method of sourcing:

Tradeshows/Conventions

For online retailers, tradeshows are a great opportunity to source goods, connect with wholesalers and manufacturers, expand their product lines, and check out new products before they even hit the market! There is a right way and a wrong way to attend tradeshows though. To get the most out of your experience, you need to prepare.

Your first step is to find the tradeshow that's right for you; there's a tradeshow for nearly every industry imaginable. One good source for locating tradeshows is www.tradeshowweek.com. Here you can search for shows alphabetically, by city and state, by industry, or by month. Tradeshows also advertise in the magazines and publications that cater to their market, and they'll give you plenty of advance notice so you can plan ahead. Another good website is www. tsnn.com.

Because real tradeshows are only open to the industry insiders, you have to register to attend. You can pre-register on a tradeshow's web site and receive your badge in the mail, which will save you a lot of time standing in line when you arrive. There's rarely any cost to register, but you will have to provide proof you're a legitimate retail business, including:

- Your business license, or tax ID
- Your resale certificate
- A photo ID
- A business card or check in your business' name

Be sure to pick up a show directory when you get there. These contain contact information for every exhibitor at the show. Most often, the phone numbers and web sites in these directories are intended for retailers only and aren't available anywhere else. While you shop around, get as many different supplier catalogs as you can, because the products on display are only a fraction of their product lines. Even if you don't see

Sourcing Tip: Three Steps to Being Prepared

When you invest time and money to attend a trade show, you want to make the most of it. That's why it is so important to be prepared. Here are some simple steps you would do well to follow:

1. Pre-register: most of these shows allow it and many require it. In addition to potential savings on registration fees, you can save yourself considerable time when you get to the convention.
2. Have productive questions ready for the exhibitors: How quickly can they deliver?, How quick are their reorders?, etc.
3. Think ahead and anticipate your needs:
   A. Pad and paper: You'll want to keep track of who impressed you.
   B. A sufficient amount of business cards: Typically an exhibitor can scan your ID badge and get all your contact information; however, if that's not the case, you want to be ready.
   C. A knapsack: You're going to be collecting information all day and carrying it around—you'll want some place to put it.

4. Have your research results handy: remember what Jen taught you during the first half of the book? Don't forget to take your list of items you're thinking about selling. Sometimes the perfect information to take to these events is your Product Expansion Schedule (see Chapter 13).

anything at their booth that interests you, they may have hundreds of other products in their catalogs that may be perfect for you.

Trade Organizations/Associations

Let's say you have a certain product niche, and you would like to locate more wholesalers. If you have difficulty with the methods above, you should investigate trade organizations. Just about every product under the sun has a trade organization or association that is comprised of leading manufacturers in that field or particular product niche.

Trade organizations are a great resource for targeted markets and are highly trustworthy. Manufacturers pay very large membership fees just to be part of these organizations. It's a point of pride and credibility for many companies and worth checking out.

Using Trade Publications - Getting Inside Information

If you're an online retailer, or any type of retailer, there's probably no better reading material for you than industry publications. What other reading will help you source and market products and build your product lines around your customers' needs?

What's a Trade Publication?

According to Lisa Suttora, of WhatDoISell.com, "A trade publication is a magazine, newspaper, or even e-mail newsletter that is written specifically for industry insiders." You can find an extremely broad range of information in a trade magazine, such as:

- The product lines that are selling
- Ways other retailers are successfully marketing their products
- Trending reports that show the influences affecting both what's being manufactured now and what's going to be selling
- Information on upcoming trade shows
- Supplier contact information
- The new products that manufacturers will be introducing
- Manufacturers' reasons for going in a particular direction, what's influencing sales, which products consumers are buying, and the factors that led them to create a product line

Invest in Knowledge

Every industry has a publication and they're only available to subscribers. Some are free while some go as high as $250 a year. But the information in them can save you a lot of trial-and-error in your product sourcing decisions. It may be worth spending the money up front, rather than trying to guess what will sell well and ending up with costly quantities of left-over inventory. To find industry publications that may be helpful, try searching the name of your industry and the term "trade publication" or "trade magazine" on Google.

What's in It for Me?

The advantage of reading trade papers is you're not blindly sourcing products. You have a foundation for making good product sourcing choices. While the research in the previous chapters helps you determine the sales trends specifically on eBay, these types of publications give you a broad look into the entire industry and trends. These publications forecast trends six to twelve months in advance, so you can see what will be selling next season and start sourcing it now. You're able to establish your corner of the market before trends reach their climax and the market becomes saturated.

Idea Sourcing

Trade magazines also help you diversify your product line. They show you numerous trends, and give you ideas and multiple ways to approach selling within your industry. "You've got to look at all the ideas available for different kinds of products to sell," says Suttora. "You can't do that in a vacuum—you need a system to help you have creative ideas."

3. Reliable Directories

Both of the methods of product sourcing I've already described are time-consuming and expensive. I should know, because that's how we created our company! They are the two methods we have been using at Worldwide Brands for the last seven years. The third method of sourcing is to use reliable directories that perform the above two methods for you.

Our Wholesale Supplier Directory, OneSource™, represents MILLIONS of brand name products that you can sell online. Over the years, we have created the most comprehensive sourcing directory for online sellers. Consider this list a background check on thousands of suppliers, manufacturers and wholesalers.

Sourcing Tip: Beware of the Search Engines!

While using search engines for finding trade magazines is a good idea, using search engines to find suppliers can be a nightmare. Here is why:

Real wholesalers don't advertise in the search engines.

Most people who sell products online automatically jump into the search engines when they're looking for wholesalers of products to sell. Believe it or not, the search engines are just about the last place you want to look.

The vast majority of real wholesale suppliers do not need (or even want) to advertise on the Internet. For the wholesale supply industry, there is an entire sales and marketing structure that has been in place forever, long before the Internet ever came to be.

Real wholesale supply companies deal for the most part with LARGE retailers: Sears, Kmart, Wal-Mart, etc. These wholesale supply companies have entire sales divisions in place, with salespeople who actually travel to and call on these massive accounts personally. That's the way it's been done for so long that legitimate wholesale suppliers take a very serious risk of hurting themselves by deviating from that strategy.

They also realize that this advertised web site approach will attract thousands of very small retailers. That means a large influx of very small accounts; accounts who will only buy a few hundred or a couple of thousand dollars worth of product at a time, not hundreds of thousands of dollars at a time.

Wholesale suppliers pay their account reps good money to bring in and work with new accounts. The larger the account, the better it is for the wholesaler. Many account reps also earn commissions from the sales they make to their accounts. So, from the wholesalers' point of view, large accounts are good and small accounts can be more time-consuming than they're worth.

This doesn't mean that there's anything wrong with small home-based Internet businesses! Again, this is simply the way most of the big wholesalers view their world, and you have to understand that in order to make progress with them.

There are many real wholesale suppliers who will work with small retailers. It's just not usually in their best interest to help you find them! The big brand name wholesalers of the world just don't go around spending time and money advertising themselves to an Internet audience that they feel won't be a significant part of their overall business.

That's why, as an online retailer, YOU have to go to them.

Fake wholesalers, however, do advertise on the search engines.

The search engine keywords "Wholesale," "Wholesale Products," "Drop Shipping," etc., attract a huge number of people who own or are starting home-based Internet businesses. That's because people who are relatively new to eCommerce are not yet aware of these wholesale scammers and sellers of sub-standard information. Most people simply do not know that the search engines are the wrong place to look for legitimate wholesalers.

While 98% of the legitimate wholesalers in the world do not advertise there, for reasons we've just discussed, those search engine keywords are the sweet spot for the middlemen, the MLM schemes, the "Get Rich Quick" con artists, and the sellers of junk information.

Through careful screening, all of our suppliers meet the following criteria:

- They will NOT charge you an account setup fee in order to do business with them.
- They are ALL genuine factory-authorized wholesalers, or sometimes the actual manufacturer of the products they sell.
- They all carry only brand new, factory warranted products.
- They have all agreed to work with home-based Internet businesses.
- They ALL KNOW that they are listed in our directory, One-Source. They are EXPECTING calls from people just like you.
- Every light bulk wholesaler we list will sell to home-based Internet businesses in affordable quantities while still providing bulk wholesale pricing.
- Every drop shipper we list will drop ship for your Internet store. They will NOT force you to buy a minimum number of products; single products sent directly to a single customer of yours are just fine with all of them.

We started compiling this directory back in 1999, when we began researching, locating and pre-qualifying genuine wholesalers that are willing and ready to work with small home-based online sellers. Of course, the purpose of this book is to educate and not self-promote, but when talking about trusted sources its important to note that Worldwide Brands is the Internet's most trusted source for genuine wholesalers. Our product sourcing education is used by eBay University, and we write and host Entrepreneur Magazine's Product Sourcing and EBiz Radio Shows. Personally, I am the official product sourcing editor for eBay Radio. In addition, our free newsletter gives you a new, free, legitimate wholesale product supplier each week. We certainly invite you to check us out at www.worldwidebrands.com.

The only other directory that we recommend you take a look at is www.thomasnet.com. It is a helpful free resource for locating manufacturers. They are essentially a business to business online directory which lists thousands of manufacturers. ThomasNet, formerly known as the Thomas Register, is a great way to gather manufacturer leads. However, ThomasNet isn't all about manufacturers of 'ready-to-sell' products. They contain huge numbers of manufacturers that produce the component parts of products, such as ball-bearings, circuit boards, plastics, etc. This means you will have to do some serious hunting in order to track down worthy candidates for your product sourcing needs.

Beware of Product Sourcing Middlemen!

Finally, when you are looking for product suppliers, you should always keep the evil middleman in mind. Whether on eBay or anywhere else, you're going to find a large number of people who are going to promise you instant riches, tell you that their "amazing systems" will make you rich overnight, and claim that they can make your online business or your wholesale product sourcing "simple."

Many of them look very legitimate. In fact, many of them are not necessarily doing anything illegal; they're just selling you information or services that really don't work.

Product sourcing middlemen have fooled tens of thousands of people into wasting millions of dollars on their schemes. Real, effective wholesale product sourcing takes patience and a commitment to learning. That's true of any legitimate business process, and we all know that. It's just common sense. Sometimes, though, common sense flies out the window when someone promises to fulfill our dreams quickly for just a few bucks.

There is an entire industry of people on the Internet that make their money by fooling you into thinking they are legitimate wholesale suppliers, when in reality they're not. These people are called product sourcing middlemen.

First, let's understand what the word "middlemen" means.

The Product Sourcing Supply Chain

The product supply chain is how a product gets from the manufacturer to the end consumer—your customer. When it's working the way it should, it goes like this:

Manufacturer → Wholesaler → Retailer → Consumer

Many people have the mistaken impression that Link Two in the chain, the wholesaler, is a middleman, because they are in the middle, between the manufacturer, and you, the retailer.

That's not true. The wholesaler, Link Two in the product supply chain, is there for a very important reason: manufacturers don't have the infrastructure to actually sell and deliver small numbers of their products directly to you, the retailer. Real wholesalers provide that infrastructure (warehouses, order systems, delivery trucks, account representatives, etc.) for the manufacturer.

So, Link Two, the wholesaler, is a legitimate wholesale supplier, not a middleman.

Here's an example of where an illegitimate middleman fits into that supply chain:

Manufacturer → Wholesaler → Middleman → Retailer → Consumer

A middleman is someone who takes your place in the product supply chain, and bumps you down a link. They try to make you believe they are Link Two in the chain (a wholesaler), when they are really Link Three (a retailer). Sometimes, it's worse than that. You could end up dealing with a fake supplier who is actually three or four links down the chain.

How does that affect you? It hits you where it hurts: right in the profit margin.

For every link you, the retailer, drop down in that chain, your "wholesale" prices go up, and you earn smaller profits. You need to be buying your products from a REAL wholesale supplier that works directly with the product manufacturer. Otherwise, your profit margin will suffer.

Tell-Tale Signs of a Middleman:

Whenever and wherever you find the name of a company that is supposed to be a wholesaler, be very careful. Learn to recognize the signs of a middleman:

- Any wholesale web site that charges you a sign-up or monthly fee IS a middleman. Real wholesalers do NOT charge monthly fees.
- Any wholesale web site that does not give you a full company name, address and phone number to call, is probably a middleman.
- Any wholesaler that does not ask you for a business license and sales tax ID is probably a middleman.
- Any wholesale web sites that make claims about how much money you can make using their service is probably a middleman.
- Any wholesale web site that makes claims about how much money they have made with their products is probably a middleman.
- Any wholesale web site that you notice is marketing exactly the same products as another supposed wholesale web site is probably a middleman.
- Any wholesale web site that tries to sell you services other than wholesale products is probably a middleman.

What Can You Do to Avoid the Middleman?

If you come across a wholesaler that you're not sure about, there are some things you can do to help you decide if they are legitimate:

- Call them. If someone answers and just says "Hello," you are not talking to a real business. You SHOULD be able to reach an operator who can direct you to an account representative. Ask the account rep all the questions you like, until you're satisfied.Go to www.whois.net and do a search on the company's web site domain name. If the results tell you that the site is registered to an individual name, chances are you're dealing with a middleman. If it's registered to a company name, that's not proof, but it's a good sign that they might be legitimate.

- Search the Internet using the web site name, and then the company name. If anyone has had trouble with them, you'll find out quickly.
- Search the Better Business Bureau web site, at www.BBB.org, for complaint history.
- Contact the Chamber of Commerce in the city or town where the business claims to be located, and ask about them. Even if they are not a chamber member, someone there should be able to give you some idea about them.

Making sure you're dealing with a real wholesaler can make or break your eBay business, so please be sure that you know who you're dealing with.

Quiz:
What is the most important thing to avoid when sourcing?

Answer:
The evil middleman! He'll drive your prices through the roof and you won't be able to compete.

How Do I Make a Deal with a Vendor?

9

Once you've done the research for the product, and found a genuine wholesaler, it's time to contact them to set up an account and get some products. The account you're trying to set up allows you to buy products from the wholesale company and resell the products at retail prices to your online store customers.

In this chapter, Robin talks about:

• Making the initial contact
• Setting up a wholesale account
• The information wholesalers need to create an account

Making the Initial Contact

Where do you start? Well, let's start by simply calling the wholesale supplier. When you get an answer, ask for the sales department. Your attitude on the phone during this first contact goes a long way toward determining whether the sales rep will give you an account.

These wholesale company reps are looking for business-like professionals to sell to. They honestly don't want to waste their time setting up an account for someone they feel isn't going to place any significant amount of orders with them. They would much rather spend their time setting up an account for someone they think is going to actually buy products, than someone whom they think is an amateur.

Remember, you are the one who needs the good will of the account rep, not the other way around.

As a home-based business owner, here are some basic guidelines that you want to follow when you call a wholesale account rep for the first time:

- Don't make "first contact" business calls from a cell phone. It's annoying to the reps that have to deal with your signal cutting in and out, and it is unprofessional.
- Quiet Please! Make sure you don't have a stereo blasting in the background, or kids screaming and running around the house, or dogs barking. You want the rep to think you're calling from an office, not a home. Offices are quiet!
- Never call with an attitude. If you act like you're doing the rep a favor by calling them, or if you act like they owe you something, the account rep will most likely blow you off after your second sentence, and then you'll have to move on to another wholesaler. This needs to be a respectful and professional business conversation. That doesn't mean you have to demean yourself in any way. Just be professional, polite, and listen when the rep is talking.

  We've spoken to many people who have asked us why they can't get accounts with wholesale companies, and while we're answering that question, they're interrupting us, and treating us like we're their indentured servants. That's their problem, right there!

Here's an opening script that we use when contacting suppliers for the first time:

> "Hello, this is Robin Cowie, President of WorldWide Brands, Inc. I'm interested in retailing your products. Can you tell me how I can set up a retail account with your company?"

Use your name, and always use your business name. If a supplier thinks for one minute that you're trying to buy products for your personal use at wholesale prices, you'll never hear from them again.

Let the sales rep tell you what they need from you on the first call. Don't ask too many questions about what you get from them yet.

Setting Up a Wholesale Account

You need to be ready to create an account during the initial contact if the opportunity is presented. You will need specific information that the account rep will want from you. Being prepared with this information will make you sound more professional and more like an experienced retailer.

What You Need

The account rep may ask you a few initial questions over the phone, or they may simply refer you to a page on their web site where you can fill out the information they need. There are still a large number of wholesale companies who don't use the Internet very efficiently, so they may ask you for a mailing address instead, and send you the forms to fill out at home, or fax them to you.

Regardless of how you submit the account setup information to them, they will all pretty much be asking for the same information. One thing you can be sure they'll want is your business name and sales tax ID number. If you come across someone claiming to be a wholesale product supplier that doesn't ask you for this information, they're not a legitimate wholesale supplier, even if they offer some explanation as to why they don't need that information.

- Your registered business name is the official name of your company. In order to do business as a retailer, you have to establish a company name and register that name with your state. This is true even if you only plan to sell on eBay auctions. Wholesalers need to have your business name on file so they have proof that you are, in fact, a real retailer, allowing them to charge you wholesale prices without charging you tax.
- Tax ID: There are two basic kinds of tax IDs. One is called an Employer Identification Number (EIN). If you start a business as a sole proprietorship, you simply file papers with your state and you're in business. You really don't need an EIN number at that point. The EIN number is usually used to report earnings that you pay to your employees. The kind of tax ID you need is a sales tax ID. Again, a real wholesaler can't sell you products at wholesale, unless you show them proof that you're authorized by your state to collect sales tax from your customers. The sales tax ID is that proof.

There are states that don't have a state sales tax. If you live in one of those states, you obviously can't get a sales tax ID from your state. However, the wholesaler will still require proof of your legal business and may ask you for an EIN or Social Security Number.

In a case like that, you can get an EIN for your legally registered business at www.irs.gov. It's free, and it doesn't take long to get. So if you're in a sales tax-free state, you should look into getting an EIN before contacting wholesalers.

Quiz:
What is the most important thing you can do in preparing to talk to a supplier?

Answer:
Become professional. Have a tax ID and a business name, and everything else that will convince the supplier that you are really serious about doing business with them.

Information Wholesalers Need to Create Your Account

The wholesale account application or account rep will probably ask you for more information pertaining to your business. This information can include your business address, phone and fax numbers, hours of operation, etc. When you're a home-based, online business, questions like these can make you nervous. Remember, wholesalers aren't always overly anxious to do business with a home-based online business.So when you complete the application, consider your answers carefully. The application should look professional, and it helps if it looks like it comes from a business location, not a home.

I'm not suggesting that you want to hide the fact that you are home-based. You'll tell the wholesaler that before your account set up is completed anyway. It just helps if you can legitimately get further into the account set up process before you have to tell them. By that time, your rep will have gotten to know you a bit and will already be feeling comfortable that you're serious about your business. He or she will have fewer concerns about your business at that point and will be much more likely to grant you an account, even if the wholesaler generally doesn't work with home-based businesses. I've seen it happen many times, and it is all based on the relationship you can build with the account rep.

If they do ask if you are home-based up front, be completely truthful with them and take your chances. The worst thing that can happen is you have to go to the next wholesaler on your list. Never mislead people that you work with in business.

Sourcing Tip: E-mailing Suppliers

Don't send out mass e-mails looking for information and accounts. Even if you use an e-mail template, send each one individually. If a wholesaler sees multiple addresses in your e-mail, they'll assume you're fishing and may not even bother responding.

If you do e-mail suppliers keep the following things in mind:

- Check your presentation: Your grammar, your punctuation, your capitalization. Almost any writing program comes with a spellchecker—use it.
- If your e-mail looks like it was written by a first-grader, a wholesaler will think you're either lazy or incompetent.
- Sign your e-mail with your name, title, and business website or name.

Here are some things to remember about the business information you put on your application.

Business Address: Your business address is, of course, your home address. If your home address is 100 Merchants Road, then it will look like you have a business office. However, if your home address is 234 Sunny Morning Way, Apartment #5, the wholesaler is going to know right away that you are a home-based business. The problem is that your application could end up being trashed before they even give you a chance. That's unfair, but it happens sometimes. You may want to consider renting a local P.O. Box in a commercial area to give your business a more professional look. They're cheap, convenient, and this isn't the only reason you'll want one. When you deal with your customers, it's better if your business address sounds business-like to them too.

Business Phone and Fax: You should put a phone number here that isn't likely to be answered by one of your kids, or by someone who simply says "Hello." When you're first starting out, I know it's hard to justify spending money on a second phone line, so in this case, you can use a cell phone number if you have one. Again, this isn't just for your wholesale account application. Anyone you deal with concerning your online business should get a business-like answer when they call you. If it's going to be your cell phone, change your cell phone's voice-mail message to something like "Thank you for calling Mary Smith of Smith Enterprises. I am currently on another line or away from my desk. Please leave a message, and I'll get right back to you." As for a fax number, if you have one, great. If you don't, just put N/A on the account application.

Hours of Operation: When you own an online business, your real hours of operation are 24/7. Keep this one simple though, and say Monday through Friday, 9 AM to 5 PM. Even if you're working your day job at that time, your account rep can still get your professional voice mail, and leave you a message.

Business Status: You might come across a wholesale account application that asks you what the status of your business is. That means they want to know if your company is a partnership, a sole proprietorship, a corporation, a retailer, etc. Sometimes your business will be more than one of those things, in which case you write them all on the application. You could be a corporation and a retailer, for example.

If you see this question on an account application, you're probably dealing with a wholesaler that is pretty demanding in their criteria for establishing accounts. That's OK, just write in the answers and keep going.

Time in Business: The wholesaler will also probably ask you how long you've been in business. If you're a new business, you have to tell them. Once again, never mislead anyone you do business with.

There will always be people out there who will tell you that a certain amount of deception and underhandedness is unavoidable in business. That's not true. On the Internet, your reputation is critically important, and if you're not always honest with everyone you deal with, people will find out. Then they'll post it all over the search engines, and everyone else will find out.

If you mislead a wholesaler and get caught later, you'll just end up running a bunch of auctions or a store that you can't get products for anymore, because the wholesaler found out you misled them, and cut you off. Sometimes they're willing to work with new or smaller businesses, sometimes they're not. You need to always tell them the truth and take your chances if you're going to establish successful business relationships.

Even so, if you've been at this for say, a few months, you probably don't want to say "four months." It is legitimate to say "less than a year." If they ask you for the date you started your business, you can just put down the year alone.

Trade and Bank References: What a wholesale account application is asking here is "What other wholesalers have you bought from in the past?"

For most home-based online business owners, that's a tough one, because it's a Catch 22. If you're trying to get set up with your first wholesaler, you don't have any trade references. But your first wholesaler may not set you up without them.

Along those same lines, they'll probably ask for business bank references. They'll want to know who you bank with and may ask you for certain business bank account information. What they're looking for is information on banks that may have extended business credit to you in the past.

So they'll want trade and bank references. Most home-based online business owners won't have those at first. But there is a completely legitimate way around those issues that works almost every time. It has to do with the reason they're asking you these questions. Most wholesalers are used to extending credit to their retailers. That means, of course, that you can place orders now and pay for them at the end of the month. It's called Net Thirty, which means you have thirty days from the order or invoice date to pay them for the products.

However, if you tell the wholesaler that you don't want credit terms, then the need for the trade and bank references goes away. You tell them that you either want to pay for the products with cash up front or by credit card, which is what the vast majority of home-based online business owners do anyway. If they don't have to process you for an extension of credit, they have a much easier time giving you an account.

Later on, when you've worked with a wholesaler for a while, you can ask them for credit, and you may get it. In fact, it is amazing how little product you need to be purchasing to secure terms of thirty days. "Thirty days same-as-cash" means that the supplier will send you the product and you pay them in thirty days. Usually you need to be purchasing at least $500 worth of product to make it worthwhile to a supplier. This wholesaler becomes your first trade reference, for when you talk to other wholesalers.

DUNS Number: For the purposes of this discussion, Dun & Bradstreet is basically a business credit reporting agency. They do much more, but the main reason a wholesaler may ask you for a DUNS number is so that they can pull a credit report on your business.

Once your legal business gets rolling, it's a good idea to look into getting a DUNS number and begin building your business credit record. At this point though, the wholesaler is asking you this for the same reason they wanted trade and bank references. They think you want them to extend a Net Thirty credit for your account.

You can make this issue go away in the same way as the other. Simply tell them you don't want Net Thirty at this time, and you will pay by credit card as you go.

Estimate Purchases from Current Suppliers: This one is fairly rare, but you may see it from time to time. A wholesaler who asks this is trying to establish potential sales that they may make to you. This number will have some effect on their decision to give you an account, but will also be used internally by the wholesaler to estimate their own quarterly sales. If you're new, and don't currently purchase from other suppliers, just write N/A here.

Product Mix: When you see this, the wholesaler is looking for information on what other products you sell. A wholesaler of candles and incense might feel like they're wasting their time setting up an account for a retailer who currently sells radio-controlled cars, for example.

Wholesalers are most interested in setting up accounts for retailers that have an established customer base which buys products related to what the wholesaler carries. This makes a wholesaler feel confi-

dent that you may be placing many large orders with them over a short period of time. That means sales, and that's what it's all about. So asking for your current product mix can be a very important question, although not all wholesalers ask it.

Size of Customer Base: Some wholesalers will be interested in your current customer base—the number of people you already sell to on a regular basis. If you're new to e-tailing and you don't have the numbers, you can always write in "New Business." Wholesalers don't

necessarily have a problem with a new business; but if they're asking this question, they are probably fairly strict about new accounts.

Physical Storefront: Sometimes you'll find wholesalers who want to see information on, or even an actual picture of, your physical storefront. That means that they want you to have a brick-and-mortar store. There are several reasons for that, but mostly it centers on product wholesalers who have physical sales territories to maintain. They can't step on the toes of those sales territories by allowing people to sell all across those territories on the Internet. If they absolutely require a physical storefront, there's no getting around it, and you should just move on to the next wholesaler on your list.

This is the basic information most wholesale suppliers will ask for in an account application. Overall, this sounds much harder than it is. Trust me, wholesale account reps are people too. Just be prepared, tell it like it is, and ask them to help.

You'll get turned down for many more wholesale accounts than you'll get accepted for. I certainly did when my online business was new. That's OK. Just move on to the next supplier on your list, and start again. You'll find good suppliers you can work with, and if you're armed with the information above, it will happen sooner than you think.

Once your account is set up, you can call and begin asking questions, such as "How soon after I place an order do you ship it?", "Do you have overnight shipping available?", and (my personal favorite), "Happy New Year, Dave; it's eighty-two degrees here in Orlando...how's the weather up there in Saskatoon?"

They'll help you with what you need. If you have questions, just ask.

However, you should not ask a supplier's sales rep technical questions about how to place products on your web site or other auctions. He or she is a salesperson, not a technical help desk. That's something you should ask the tech support people at your Internet store's hosting company, or at eBay. Remember, a wholesaler is your supplier, not your business coach. They have limited time and manpower, so don't expect them to hold your hand and advise you on how to run your eBiz, optimize your site, or improve your traffic. They aren't there to answer questions you ought to be researching on your own time.

Not every wholesaler will be taking new accounts, and not every supplier will be willing to work with home-based businesses. But many are, and by being professional and prepared, you can greatly increase your success with them.

Quiz:
Will all suppliers work with small home based online sellers?

Answer:
No! Many will not. Don't be discouraged—more and more will.

What are the Types of Supplier Relationships?

10

One of the keys to effective product sourcing is understanding the different kinds of relationships a retailer can have with a supplier. In this chapter, Robin explores the pros and cons of each of the following different, basic types of supplier relationships:

• Drop shipping
• Light bulk wholesale
• Liquidation and closeout
• Importing
• Large volume wholesale

Understanding Product Distribution

People have been distributing products since before the first mastodon skinner traded a fur coat for a flint axe.

Here's how it works:

Let's say ABC Manufacturers makes a product called Mom's Ankle Wax. We'll say that Mom's Ankle Wax has been around for years. It's a very well-known brand name product. It will—without a doubt—give you the shiniest ankles on your block, and everybody wants some. (I'm painting a nice picture for you, aren't I?!)

The problem? ABC Manufacturers makes Mom's Ankle Wax, but they don't sell it directly to the public. They're a manufacturing operation. They're far too busy melting paraffin and waxing test ankles to go around building stores all over the place. They need distributors—companies who will take their product and distribute it to the places that will sell it.

For years, ABC Manufacturers has sold Mom's Ankle Wax to a company called DEF Distributors. The founder of DEF Distributors knew Mom herself, back in the old days when she made her Ankle Wax by hand, out in the turkey barn. Today, DEF Distributors buys Mom's Ankle Wax by the truckload. They pay $5.00 a case for it, which is a very good price. It's such a good price, it has its own name: the Manufacturer's Wholesale Price.

However, DEF Distributors does not sell it to the general public either. They are a distributor. They distribute Mom's Ankle Wax to the retailer.

DEF Distributors works with a chain of retail stores called Wax 'R Us. This place was founded by a retail business visionary who saw the incredible potential of Mom's Ankle Wax a long time ago. Today, Wax 'R Us retail stores line every street corner in every major city in the country. Wax 'R Us buys truckloads of Mom's Ankle Wax from DEF Distributors for $10.00 a case.

So DEF Distributors makes $5.00 on every case of Mom's Ankle Wax they sell to Wax 'R Us retail stores. This makes DEF Distributors very happy.

Cases and cases of Mom's Ankle Wax arrive in the stockrooms of Wax 'R Us stores everywhere. The Wax 'R Us employees open those cases, and pull twelve cans of Mom's Ankle Wax out of each case. With their pricing guns, they stick a price of $4.50 on each and every can.

Wax 'R Us stores make a total of $44.00 on each case of Mom's Ankle Wax. (12 cans x $4.50 per can = $54.00, minus the $10.00 they paid for the case = $44.00).

Wax 'R Us is even happier than DEF Distributors.

However, the happiest people of all are the people who can stroll into Wax 'R Us and purchase a can of Mom's Ankle Wax for only

$4.50. They think this is a great price, and they're walking around with the shiniest ankles in town.

Well, that's it…basic product distribution. The manufacturer sells to the distributor, the distributor sells to the retailer, and the retailer sells to the end user (the customer). The manufacturer, the distributor and the retailer all make money because the customer is willing to spend money for the product.

In Chapter 8, we talked about the manufacturer-distributor-retailer relationship. When you use suppliers to sell products on the Internet (or anywhere else), YOU become the RETAILER in that relationship.

Drop Shipping Pros and Cons: the Cost of Convenience

Many online sellers tout drop shipping for its ease; others dismiss it, arguing it leaves no room for profit. Like every other product sourcing method, drop shipping brings its own unique set of advantages and drawbacks to your eBiz.

The Basics

Drop shipping is a service some wholesale distributors provide that enables you to sell items on your website without physically stocking them. The wholesaler stocks large quantities of product, which you list in your web store. Customers place their orders with you, the retailer, and you pass them on to the drop shipper. The drop shipper sends the product directly to your customers, but remains invisible to them. The end result is that you charge the retail price and, after you have processed the order with your customer, pay the wholesaler the wholesale price.

The Upside

Drop shipping presents your business with numerous benefits:

- **Lower overhead.** The costs that go into warehousing and shipping individual items can be tremendous. It doesn't become efficient to do so until you do it on a large enough scale.
- **No inventory investments.** You don't pay the wholesaler for an order until your customer pays you. And you can test new products without purchasing inventory that may not sell.
- **Recovered time.** The time you spent receiving and organizing inventory, printing labels, and packing and shipping orders is time you can now spend promoting your web site and providing faster customer service.

- **No order minimums.** Your wholesale orders are based on your customers' orders. You can order as many or few items as you need—even down to individual products.
- **Broader product selection.** You can carry items in your product line-up that would be difficult to physically stock; you're also able to offer large items, such as furniture, without the hassle of trying to ship each piece.

The Downside

Of course, drop shipping has limitations—two in particular:

- **Thinner profit margins.** Wholesale is a volume business—the more you buy, the better your price per-piece. Although your drop ship prices are true wholesale prices, they are wholesale prices on one item. You're not receiving additional discounts for buying bulk, so your per-item costs are naturally higher. You're also paying a drop ship fee, either per container or per unique shipping location, to cover the extra labor and material costs the drop shipper incurs.
- **Occasional delivery issues.** If your drop shipper is slow filling your orders, or does a poor job packaging them, it reflects badly on you and costs you repeat business. When using a new supplier, it's always a good idea to test them out first and get an idea of what your customers will experience. Place an order with them yourself, and see how quickly and competently they handle it. If you order a few of your most popular items, you'll also have them on hand in case your drop shipper ever runs short or somehow drops the ball.

The Bottom Line

Especially when you're getting started, drop shipping is an easy, cost-effective tool for your eBiz. That doesn't mean you should limit yourself to using only drop shipping. The most successful retailers use multiple product sourcing techniques. Drop shipping is a great complement to your other product sourcing methods, and should be a part of your overall product sourcing strategy.

When you're just starting out, or you are wanting to test new product lines, but don't want to spend your own money up front for those products just in case they don't sell, then a drop shipper is a good choice to go with.

In product sourcing, you need to decide whether you're going to spend money buying bulk quantities of products from wholesalers, storing them at your house, and shipping them to your customers yourself. The deciding factor is usually how well you think the products will sell.

Using drop shippers allows you to sell brand new, brand name products to your customers without paying for those products before you sell them.

Light Bulk Wholesaling

Another supplier relationship for your home-based, Internet business is to buy "in bulk" from wholesale suppliers.

The Basics

This means, of course, that you find a wholesale supplier, and spend some money up front buying a few cases of products. The wholesale supplier ships those products to you. You stash those cases of products in your garage or spare room, and repack and ship each product individually to your customers.

The Upside
- **Better Pricing:** Since you are ordering in quantity, even though it's small quantity, you will get wholesale price discounts. These discounts make the per-item wholesale cost less than what you would pay if you were having the product single item drop shipped.

- **Inventory Control:** You can effectively avoid over-selling or back ordering products because you are actually stocking/maintaining your own inventory.

The Downside
- **Risking Bad Product Choices:** You have to research what you are going to sell. New sellers, who purchase in light bulk and don't do their research, sometimes get stuck with products they have trouble selling. Remember Jen's example in Chapter 3, where a lady bought a large supply of women's jeans that would not sell? Market research is very important!
- **Extra Work:** There is more work involved in stocking and maintaining your own inventory, but the majority of the work will come when it's time to ship. With light bulk orders, you will be packaging and shipping products and sending them out directly to your customers yourself.
- **Most Real Wholesale Suppliers Won't Work with You:** it's unfortunate, but true. Most legitimate wholesale suppliers out there do not want to sell bulk orders of products to small, home-based Internet businesses. Why? Because they don't have the money to order thousands of dollars worth of products at one time.

You see? A wholesale supplier's business is based on volume sales. They don't make very much of a profit on the products they wholesale. That means that they have to sell a lot of product in order to make money. So a wholesale supplier's main business is selling truckloads of products to large retail chains, like Sears®, Target®, KMart®, etc. They simply won't sell to anyone who can't afford to place a minimum order ranging from $5,000 to $25,000, or so. They don't consider it to be worth their effort!

The Solution
Over the years, my company has become very well known in the wholesale industry, because we've not only helped small business owners to connect with suppliers, but we've also brought a great deal of business to many wholesale suppliers from small businesses.

Because we have that reputation, we are able to go to large whole-sale suppliers and say, "Look, there are a lot of small businesses out there who want to buy in bulk, but can't afford your high minimums. If you're willing to lower your minimums to an affordable level for us, we will get your company's name out to many home-based Internet businesses that want to buy from you." Well, the wholesale suppliers know us, and they like the idea that we can bring them your business without costing them any advertising money on their end. It's truly a win-win situation for everyone.

"Light bulk" wholesaler is a term that we created to describe a real wholesale supplier that will:

- Sell new, factory-warranted products, at wholesale pricing, to the home-based Internet business owner.
- Sell to you in affordable quantities, with minimum orders under $500. That's why we call it "light bulk." Our research team has spoken personally with each and every one of the thousands of wholesale suppliers in our directory. They are all willing to do business with you on the terms above. Their contact information is updated constantly, and our team adds new wholesale suppliers on a daily basis.

Your Process for Working with Light Bulk Wholesalers

1. Once you find a light bulk wholesaler you want to work with, call them and set up a free account, to start buying from them.
2. You'll need to prepare your packing and shipping workspace. A spare room, a basement, or a garage usually works best, but many people do this right in their living rooms. You'll need:

- Some kind of organized shelving, where you can place your products. You'll want to label the shelves with the product names and stock numbers.
- Shipping materials, such as properly-sized boxes, shipping bags, shipping tape, some bubble-wrap plastic or Styrofoam peanuts, etc. Your wholesale supplier will be able to give you the sizes of the shipping boxes or bags you'll need to ship each individual product.
- An Inbox and an Outbox, or something similar, so you can physically keep track of which orders still need to be filled, and which are already done.

- A shipping label printer. The best way to go here is to contact UPS (at UPS.com) and set up a "Daily Pickup" shipping account with them. When you do that, they will supply you with FREE "UPS Worldship" software for your computer. That software actually connects to UPS over the Internet, and calculates your shipping costs for each item you send. You can ship by UPS ground, air, or overnight—any way your customer wants to ship the product. It also keeps a record of your shipments, your tracking numbers, and much more. It prints all your official UPS shipping labels too, so that all you have to do is slap that label on your package, and you're done! UPS will "rent" you a shipping label printer for only about $4 a month, and provide you with all the FREE shipping labels and other supplies you need for that printer. Setting up a UPS account is cheap, and it really saves you a great deal of hassle.

3. After you do some market research (explained in the previous chapters), you decide which products you want to sell online, and place an order for those products.
4. After the cases of products arrive at your home, the first thing you need to do is inspect those products! Open the cases, and take all the products out. Do a quick inspection for signs of obviously broken or damaged products. Damaged products are rare, but you do need to find out right away if all the products you have are in good shape. If you do find one or two that are damaged, the sooner you tell your wholesaler, the better. They will work out a replacement arrangement for you that won't cost you anything.
5. Place images and descriptions (you'll get these from your wholesaler) on your Internet store or auctions—and you're ready to go!

Remember that when you're shipping products to your customers yourself, you should never let more than forty-eight hours go by before you ship each product. Customer service is very important in your home-based Internet business—you need to be sure to keep your customers happy!

Light bulk wholesaling works well, and is a low-cost entry into the world of buying wholesale products in bulk. Supplementing your product sourcing with light bulk (low minimum order) wholesalers should be a part of your sourcing efforts, especially if you plan to sell in a price-driven marketplace like eBay.

Liquidation/Overstocks/ Closeouts

Companies choose to liquidate products for many reasons. It's a good idea to know why the items you're interested in are being liquidated. There may be a perfectly valid reason, but you don't want to get stuck with goods you can't sell.

Sometimes, the products being liquidated are brand new and a manufacturer simply made too many of them. Or they weren't that great of a seller to begin with, and the manufacturer or wholesaler got stuck with a lot of extras.

In our experience with liquidation, brand new products that are still in the box are more the exception than the rule. So while liquidation buying can be effective, you have to be very careful to be sure you know what you're getting.

So what exactly are you looking for? You want to find off-price, overstocks, out-of-season, promotional liquidated products. You can look at courts dealing with bankruptcy and insurance companies dealing with excess and damaged merchandise. Sometimes U.S. Customs

Sourcing Tip: Interesting Liquidation Facts*

- 4-6% of retail merchandise sold per year is returned to brick-and-mortar stores. In 2006, the National Retail Federation recorded almost 9% of holiday purchases were returned. This is even higher for online merchants.
- Product life cycles have shrunk from years to months, or even weeks, in hot consumer electronics categories.
- Studies show that the average consumer in the U.S. will struggle for twenty minutes to get a consumer electronic device working before giving up and returning it to the store.
- The federal government disposes of an average of 10,000 computers per week.

*Source: Liquidation.com presentation at eBay Live 2007

will have unclaimed goods, or the police will have stolen property you can purchase at deep discounts.

If you are careful, liquidation buying can be a good supplement to your product sourcing efforts, especially since you can use low-cost items you bought at liquidation prices to entice customers into your online store to see your more expensive (and higher profit) items. And as with any product sourcing method, when you buy liquidated goods, it's critical that you know whether or not your supplier is legitimate.

Importing

As your eBiz grows, and housing large stores of inventory becomes feasible, importing becomes a cost-effective way to source products.

According to Peter Zapf, of GlobalSources.com and GlobalSourcesDirect.com, there are several steps you should take to find and select a manufacturer to import goods:

Research Your Importers

- **Locate suppliers.** Look for online sites that deliver imported goods directly, or that list manufacturer names and contact information. If possible, attend an overseas tradeshow, visit their booths, and ask questions in person.
- **Verify suppliers.** To ensure you're dealing with legitimate suppliers, find out what steps a web site takes to authenticate the manufacturers they list. Also, ask the suppliers if they participate in any tradeshows, and then go to the shows' web sites and confirm their participation. Most tradeshows research the manufacturers they let in; and a company that invests the money to take part in a tradeshow is probably genuine. Finally, always be certain they provide you with the paperwork to prove they have all relevant certifications.
- **Evaluate suppliers.** Suggests Zapf, "Notice the customer service you receive—how long does it take them to respond to your inquiries? Are their answers thorough and friendly? If they seem capable, try them out with a small order. If you're happy, go from there."

Take steps to ensure product quality
- Request a sample, and study the product and packaging. Make sure the information and spelling are correct, and check the instructions. You don't want to find they're written in British English for a U.S. market.
- Keep in constant communication with your supplier. E-mail digital pictures back and forth of any changes.
- With a larger order, you may consider hiring a third-party quality control firm to inspect and count your products at the factory, and perform a functional check.

Large Volume Wholesalers

At Worldwide Brands, we use the term "large volume wholesaler" to describe a wholesale company that does not "drop ship" OR "light bulk" wholesale. Rather, they are companies that we have investigated and found to be legitimate wholesalers who sell in larger bulk quantities, but are willing to make deals with you on an individual basis.

Large volume wholesalers are VERY important to your overall product sourcing success. It's also important to realize that if you deal DIRECTLY with REAL drop shippers and light bulk wholesalers, THEY are all actually general wholesalers as well. They're general wholesalers who are ALSO willing to drop ship and sell in light bulk quantities, that's all. They will all be happy to give you better price breaks if you buy larger quantities from them, to round out a product line that sells well for you.

In large volume wholesaling, the wholesaler sells you cases of products, not just one of this, and one of that.

For example, when ABC Wholesale orders products from a manufacturer like First Sporting Goods, the products arrive at ABC Wholesale's warehouse in something called case lots. That just means that when the wholesaler gets them from the manufacturer, they're packed a certain number of products to a case. Some of the larger products come packed two or four to a case. Smaller ones come packed six, twelve, twenty-four, or more to a case.

If ABC Wholesale is going to sell those products to you, the retailer, at a very low 8% profit margin, then they have to sell them to you in those same cases they were packed in when they arrived in ABC Wholesale's warehouse. The wholesaler MUST be able to take

those factory-supplied cases of products, put your shipping address on them, and send them right back out the door in the same case boxes they came in. Here's why ... if ABC Wholesale has to break open those cases and repackage a half of a case, or a quarter of a case, they have to pay their employees more money to do that, because it takes them more time.

When it takes the wholesaler's employees more time, it costs the wholesale company more money, and they make less profit. Operating, for example, on an 8% profit margin, they can't afford to make less profit! So when you buy in bulk from a wholesale supplier, you're buying cases of products, packaged just as they come from the manufacturer. In order for ABC Wholesale to afford to sell to you in bulk at the low profit margins they make on most of their products, they have to require a minimum order. When you order in bulk from ABC Wholesale, your first order must be at least $500.

However, with a $500 order, they must charge you 2% over that standard 8% profit margin, which brings their profit margin to 10%. If they didn't make 10% on a $500 order, they couldn't remain in business. Remember, that's only $50 they're making on that whole order! In order for ABC Wholesale to sell to you in bulk exactly at the manufacturer's suggested wholesale price, they require that each order must be $1,000 or more. That's the minimum order they're willing to accept in order to sell to you at their standard markup of 8%.

Of course, if you happen to order some of the few products that ABC Wholesale carries that they get factory key pricing on, they make a better profit on part of your order, and that's really how wholesale suppliers pay the bills and stay in business. Most wholesale suppliers only get key pricing from the manufacturer on a small percentage of the products they carry.

Let's imagine for a moment that a wholesaler selling in bulk didn't require a minimum order. Let's say that they took your order for just two of their less expensive purple widgets, and sold them to you at manufacturer's suggested wholesale price. The purple widgets come to the wholesaler from the manufacturer, packed forty-eight to a case. For the wholesaler to get just two of those purple widgets to you, one of their employees would have to break open a case of the widgets. He would have to take two of those purple widgets out of the case box and repackage them in a smaller box.

Where does that smaller box come from? The wholesaler has to buy it separately. How about the extra packing materials that will be needed? The wholesaler has to buy those separately as well. And what about the employee's extra time? That's the costliest thing of all for the wholesale supplier!

Sourcing Tip: Math lesson

If a wholesaler sold you just two of those purple widgets, at the actual manufacturer's suggested wholesale price of $18 each, they'd make about $2.88 at that 8% profit margin. The extra shipping materials and their employee's time to repackage that order cost them about $10. The wholesaler just lost $7.12 on that one order. Obviously, they couldn't stay in business long if they did that!

When a wholesaler sells cases of products to you in bulk, though, at the minimum order amounts they require, the profit they earn makes it worthwhile enough for them to do it close to, or at, the manufacturer's suggested wholesale price. They don't have to break open the cases in their warehouse, and it doesn't cost them extra for more packing materials and extra employee time. That's what bulk wholesaling is, and that's why you see minimum order requirements from nearly all legitimate wholesalers when you buy in bulk.

Multiple Product Sourcing Relationships

No SINGLE product sourcing method will make you truly successful. Using only one sourcing method is like driving a car with only one wheel. Four wheels work much better ...

- Drop shipping works well, but has its limits, which include slimmer profit margins and occasional delivery problems. Drop shipping should be a part of your product sourcing, but not all of it.
- Bulk wholesaling works well, but most wholesalers have very high minimum orders. Supplementing your product sourcing with light bulk (low minimum order) wholesalers should be a part of your sourcing efforts.
- General wholesaling works well as an expansion tool. When your drop shipping and light bulk sourcing identify products that sell well, you can work with general wholesalers to get larger quantities of those products at better prices and increase your profit margin. When used properly, this method is a part of the whole.
- Liquidation and overstock sourcing work well, but they are not renewable sources. Once a liquidation lot is gone, it's gone. If you find a product that sells well, you'll run out of it sooner or later. That's why you need other sourcing methods: so you can find renewable sources of those products once you identify them.
- Importing works well, but it's very expensive to bring products into your country from overseas on your own. Finding importers who have already brought the products in is very important here. You can use case lots of imported goods to supplement your existing steady stream of regular products.

Successful product sourcing is the art of using a combination of tools and sources to find the right balance of product sources for your eBiz.

Here's a professional sourcing formula that works! Start with drop shipping to test product ideas, incorporate light bulk orders so you can increase your profit margin on hot sellers, and move to large volume wholesale when you find products that sell very well! Use liquidation, imports, and local sources to find extremely cheap products you can offer as 'loss leaders' to entice customers to visit your store!

Quiz:
What is the most effective product sourcing relationship?

Answer:
All of them combined. It allows for the most flexible and profitable online company.

Section 4

Sell—Like Mad!

"We have technology, finally, that for the first time in human history allows people to really maintain rich connections with much larger numbers of people."

—*Pierre Omidyar, eBay founder and Internet Entrepreneur*

How Sourcing Strategy Affects Sales

11

Now that Jen has guided you through what to look for in a marketplace and demonstrated the importance of research, and I've taken you through the best sourcing techniques and explained the various sourcing relationships, you should be adequately equipped to perform successfully on eBay. But now it's time we added some chain saws and flaming torches to the juggling mix!

This chapter is dedicated to the strategies that will truly build the profit centers into your eBay business. If you understand these concepts and use the tools that Jen and I have mentioned so far in this book, you will be mesmerized by the results.

In this chapter, Robin talks about:
• Looking for emerging markets
• Becoming a trend spotter
• Learning from your own sales
• Selling what sells, not just what's cool
• The long tail of product sourcing

Looking for Emerging Markets

An emerging market is one in which the bid rate is growing at a greater rate than the listing rate. Unlike a hot market that has reached its capacity, an emerging market still has room for growth. Don't chase after hot-ticket items within saturated markets. You're looking for neglected niche markets with greater demand than supply.

Every product has a life cycle—an item is introduced, it grows, it hits product maturity, and it begins to decline. Jen discussed this in great detail in Chapter 6. That's why it's important you know when to move on.

- Don't get carried away with fads.
- Don't try to keep up with every hot-ticket item.
- Do know about changes in your market that affect you.
- Do keep abreast of trends and make adjustments as needed.

Every large retailer follows these guidelines and they're no less important for you and your eBiz.

Sourcing Tip: When Should I Drop a Product?

- Look at what your sales numbers are telling you—sometimes sales drop for a previously popular item. It may be seasonal, or there may be greater supply in that market than before. Research will help you discover these trends.
- If new competition comes in with a lower price, you can try to out-sell them by providing more value—a better website, better customer service, etc. People will pay a bit more if they feel you're competent and trustworthy.
- Sometimes, someone has too much buying power for you to compete—that's when you need to walk away. If you find a particular product isn't selling anymore because a big competitor has come in, go find another product that's niche-oriented and that your customers will buy.

What is a Trend?

A trend is not a group of popular items that everyone is buying. A trend is an expression of what matters to consumers at the moment—it's a sign of which they're excited about. A trend can actually give you many ideas of what products might be popular in certain groups. The trend towards natural living, for example, could inspire a whole line of products because that's what people are concerned with and are thinking about. Trends grow and evolve and morph, but they have rhyme and reason—unlike fads, they don't just come out of nowhere.

Look for a definable group of customers that you can get coming back time and time again. Don't source products in a vacuum. By understanding what types and groups of products people are looking for, you will save a lot of time by making sourcing decisions that complement a group of products.

How Do I Become a Trend Spotter?

Spotting trends is a learned ability—and it doesn't require you to be trendy. It requires discipline. Make it a habit to research trends daily. There are many avenues you can use to help you research:

- Most major search engines offer keyword tracking tools that show you how many people are searching for a given item. Worldwide Brands' product sourcing tool, OneSource, includes a built-in market research function that can show you how likely a product is to sell successfully online, based on market statistics.
- In-depth trend spotting in the eBay marketplace requires a tool like HammerTap.
- The media can provide some really valuable trending stats. For example, newspapers often provide numbers and demographics for shifting trends. Look for indicators of growth and decline. You want to get in on the upswing of a trend—not when it's on its way out. Document everything so that you have it all in front of you and don't forget anything important when you sit down to analyze the results of your research.
- Consumer publications are designed around niche products, niche hobbies, and niche markets. These are a terrific resource for building niche product lines.
- Talk to the salespeople at malls and brick-and-mortar stores to find out what is selling.
- Check out trend-spotting web sites, such as www.trendwatcing.com, www.influxinsights.com, and www.trendhunter.com.
- The entertainment industry is perhaps the greatest trend set-

Tip

Quiz:
What is the best rule of thumb when thinking about trends?

Answer:
Get in early and leave before the party is over. Make sure you do your research!

ter itself. Movies and TV drive product trends. If you know what is coming out in the movie industry, you can start sourcing related products before the trends begin. A great source, www.imdb.com, maintains a list of movies that are going to be released in the coming year. So if you know now that a particular movie is going to be coming out, you can start stocking up on relevant products before they become pricey—such as Batman, Superman, Curious George, and Star Wars.

• The key is to be consistent and do your research daily. Trending information is not something you do once and then stop. Every successful business owner is going to continually be reinventing their product line on an ongoing basis. Another great website to learn more about spotting trends is Lisa Suttora's **www.whatdoisell.com**.

What Can You Learn from Your Own Product Sales?

Everyone's constantly after new products to sell, but it is just as crucial to recognize how your current products are selling. In order to know your best business move, you need to ask the right questions: What's selling? Why is it selling? When does it sell best? How frequently do my customers buy from me? Just once? Weekly? Monthly?

Sourcing Tip: When Should I Add a Product?

• If you find a product that complements your current line-up, test it out with your existing customer base and see how it sells.

• Be sure your product extensions make sense with what you're already selling—don't add snow pants to your footwear site.

• Another thing to watch is the cost—if you sell items in the $10 range, you're selling to a particular audience. By adding an item—even a related item—that's $100, you're now targeting a completely different market.

• Make sure your goods are similar in taste and price range.

• An effective product expansion schedule (see Chapter 13) is a great tool in planning the addition of new products to your inventory.

To find answers to these questions:

1. Create an Excel spreadsheet for your customers.
2. Create a customer number for every new person who buys from you.
3. Record which products they buy, when they buy, and the frequency with which they buy them.

Within a couple of months, you should see some patterns in terms of which products are being bought, how many are being bought at a time, and the things you need to know from a statistical sense to make some decisions about your products.

You can also use your research tool to research your own eBay seller ID and see all your sales data on eBay or using a research tool, like HammerTap. Keeping a close eye on your own sales will help you successfully phase out slow sellers while phasing in the new, more profitable products.

Sell What Sells, NOT What's Cool

I've been at this for years and have become very successful with my own Internet business. But let's face it, folks, if I knew what was going to sell well on the Internet tomorrow, next week, or next month, I wouldn't be writing this book! I would have retired and purchased a small private island by now.

In the retail business, whether you are online, in a physical store, in the local mall, or at a roadside stand, it makes no difference: choosing the products you are going to sell is always the hardest part of success.

I can't whip out a crystal ball and tell you what to sell. However, I can tell you about the biggest mistakes that I see new home-based Internet businesspersons making, all the time.

Too many of them want to sell what they think is cool. Of course it's always more fun to sell stuff that you are interested in, but if it doesn't sell, then you've got problems. In the previous research chapters, you learned how to find products that sell and that make you a profit.

Sadly, too many people skip that part and go right for the product, with the notion that "anything sells on eBay!" I sure don't want YOU to fall into this category. So let's walk through a little self-evaluation to make sure you are not like those who won't touch anything "not cool" with a ten-foot pole.

These types of people are fixated on four things:

- Selling only products they like.
- Selling only products they know a lot about.
- Selling only products they think are "cool" or "sexy."
- Selling only products they think are "the hottest products on the Internet."

Let's walk through some of these to see if you are headed in the right direction. Every so often, I get a few basic e-mails from people who are stuck in this rut, only wanting to sell what's cool, and I can pretty much tell what their problem is, right from the start, by the way their e-mails begin.

Let's look at a few examples. They are really quite humorous.

An email from a person who thinks they can only sell what they like starts something like this:

> "Dude, I'm like, a sk8ter, and I need to find a wholesale supplier for, like, sk8tboards + wheels + stuff."

The first problem this person is going to run into (aside from the fact that he needs to learn how to write a business e-mail!) is a problem for all four types of people here. There simply may not be a wholesale supplier for the products they want, that will work with a home-based Internet business.

The second problem is "tunnel vision." This person may actually find a wholesale supplier for "sk8tboards + wheels + stuff," and if he does, great. However, someone who has such a narrow vision of the Internet marketplace will never branch out and fulfill his own potential in that marketplace.

Say he does find the wholesale supplier he's looking for, and opens a store. Because of the narrow vision that led him there, he's likely to stick with that store, and that store alone. He'll make some money, but unless he gets really lucky, he won't make a really good income out of it. He'll piddle along selling "sk8tboard" stuff forever, when he could have done so much more.

What he needs to do is broaden his scope. It's fine if he's interested in "sk8ting," but instead of focusing on just that, he should explore selling all kinds of sporting goods.

Sam Walton, the revered founder of Wal-Mart®, was once a starting quarterback on his high school football team in Columbia, Missouri. He also liked to play basketball. Can you imagine what would have happened if Sam Walton never tried to sell anything besides football and basketball equipment? There would probably be a pretty big store in the U.S. selling just footballs and basketballs today, because Walton was a very good retailer. But it never would have grown to the size and scope of Wal-Mart today if Sam had allowed tunnel vision to crowd his overall view.

An email from a person who only thinks they can sell what's "cool" goes like this:

> "Hi, I'm looking for a wholesale supplier of electronics, like MP3 players, plasma TVs and such. Please tell me where to find them."

A request for a wholesale supplier of electronics is a dead give-away. Almost everybody who starts a home-based Internet business wants to sell electronics at first. It's the cool, sexy market, and even if you never sell anything, you can show your friends your site and say, "Dude, I can get you an xlent deal on the hottest new stuff!"

Electronics, like any other cool or sexy market on the Internet, is not the place for most people to start. That market is absolutely flooded with other people who already had the same idea, and the profit margins have plummeted. Why?

Too many inexperienced Internet sellers are trying to sell the same things. They start price wars, figuring they're going to clean up by under-cutting everyone else's prices by a little bit. Problem is, the second guy comes along and undercuts the first one a bit. Then the third person comes along and undercuts the second. And so on. Pretty soon all you have left are tens of thousands of people trying to sell electronics for pennies more than what they paid for them, just to advertise a slightly better price than their competition.

In case you've missed the point, this is NOT good. The person who wants to sell cool and sexy stuff needs to understand that they are not out here to look cool or sexy. They're here to make money. Four-slice toasters and propane camp stoves aren't sexy, but they sell and their markets are not overcrowded, and that's what the goal is.

Finally, an e-mail from a person who thinks they need to sell only the hottest products on the Internet goes like this:

> "Hello, can you tell me where I can find out what the top-selling products on eBay are? I want to know what everyone else is selling and get in on it."

BAD IDEA! Look at it this way: If you were in a giant field filled with nothing but concession stands selling salted peanuts, what's the smartest thing you could do? Set up yet another salted peanuts stand, or set up a lemonade stand?

I'd sell lemonade, wouldn't you?

In our business, we look at the lists of top-selling products on the Internet, too. Jen taught you how to do this in Chapter 3. But you don't want to be just another face in the crowd selling the same thing as everyone else. You want to think about products that may be complementary to the hottest sellers, that not many other people are selling.

If everyone and their grandmothers are selling salted peanuts, you want to be the one selling lemonade. (Or that fancy ankle wax I mentioned earlier!)

Don't Forget about the Competition

So you passed the self-evaluation and you're not a "sk8ter" looking to sell only the coolest products ever. But, just because you're not competing with all those "sk8ters" doesn't mean you don't have to compete. In Chapter 4, Jen taught you how to find your potential for sales within a particular market. Along with doing the research, you need to ask yourself these questions about the products you are considering competing with outside of eBay:

- How much competition will I have? You can find your competition the same way your customers do—type the name of your item into a search engine and sift through the results. If the market's flooded, be willing to keep looking—there are plenty of product markets out there with enough room for you.
- Can I be competitive? Consider your competition's retail prices and their shipping costs. They may offset the one with the other, so it's important to look at both. Compare them with your own wholesale and shipping costs, and determine if you'll be able to charge competitive prices and still make a profit.

The Long Tail of Product Sourcing

Chris Anderson, the Editor-in-Chief of Wired Magazine, has written an amazingly influential book on the impact of the Internet on commerce called The Long Tail. (Learn more about it at **www.thelongtail.com**).

Essentially his premise is that the future of selling is selling more of less. If you were to graph demand for any marketplace, you would find that popular, higher-demand products make up the "head" of the graph on the left, with lower-demand products trailing down to the right, forming the "tail."

Because retail chains have limited shelf space, they carry only those faster-selling products so they can turn their inventory over again and again. They don't have room to waste on products that don't cater to the mainstream market. For example, Wal-Mart is the nation's top music retailer, but they carry less than 3% of all music available to be sold.

Because of the limitless "shelf space" of the Internet, this presents a lucrative opportunity for you, as an Internet seller, to sell more of less (the items that really are the niche products.) These products that comprise the market's "tail" tend to do better online. You have the potential to offer a huge diversity of products, and you don't even have to stock them yourself. You can use drop shipping to identify which products sell extremely well, and then buy those in bulk for even greater profit margins.

And you don't have to be a big player to get the entire market for more specialized products. You actually have a greater opportunity to reach your potential leads than the larger retailers because they aren't specifically going after those tiny niche markets. You also have the

Quiz:

What's so important about the long tail of product sourcing?

Answer:

Opportunity! Never before can a single entrepreneur reach potential buyers around the world with very, very specific products. Niche the niche!

ability to reach a wider audience than even chain stores because you
have the search engines helping people find you, and sites like eBay
bringing you a funnel of traffic.

eBay Wants You to Succeed!

Don't forget that eBay makes more money if your transactions are
successful.

Consequently there are some free eBay tools that help you spot and
stay on top of trends and hot-selling products. (Remember, don't always try to sell the hot-selling product. Think of the lemonade and
peanuts example.) Here are a few of eBay's free resources:

We've already mentioned the challenges to hot lists, but that being
said, eBay's hot items list is one of the best around. Every month they
put out a new list based on their own data research. So essentially,
they're doing a large part of your market research for you, at no cost.
You can find this information at www.eBay.com/sellercentral—just
download the hot list PDF file.

For many product categories, the winter holiday season is the
make-or-break time of year. eBay puts out a couple of very specific
lists for this time of year. The holiday hot list
(**http://pages.ebay.com/sellercentral/holidayhotlist/**) and the holiday
catalog (**http://pages.ebay.com/catalog/**). The holiday catalog goes
out to eBay's top buyers, filled with buyer recommendations. However, it may prove even more useful to eBay's smart sellers. What
better way to get product sourcing ideas than to see what items eBay
is promoting to their top buyers?

The Final Word on Sourcing Strategy

Sourcing strategy is so important to us that we built research into our OneSource tool. It breaks down a product's demand, competition, advertising, and market price, and analyzes those numbers to tell you exactly what your chances are of successfully selling a given product online. It does not replace the in-depth eBay marketplace data that a research tool like HammerTap provides, but it does offer another check into why you are choosing the products you want to sell. At the end of the day, it is the people who ask the most penetrating market research questions and do the most thorough, multi-faceted product sourcing that will be the most successful sellers.

Selling Strategies for High Performance

12

You've identified products that will sell and found an excellent source for them (following Robin's excellent guidelines, of course). Now that you have what you know will sell, it's time to find out how to sell it.

The trouble is, there are so many listing choices, like:

- On what day should I end my listing?
- What time of day should I end it?
- How long should I list it?
- What listing type should I choose?
- What promotional features should I invest in to boost my selling success (i.e., highlight, bold, and etc.)?
- What price should I start with?
- What category should I put it in? And should I choose a secondary category?

The challenge is to make the right combination of selling choices to get the best possible outcome—the one that matches your selling goals. There are two ways to do this: trial and error, and research.

During this chapter, Jen talks about:
- Making the right combination of choices with research
- Three selling strategies
- Selling a higher volume
- Increasing your sales price per listing
- Balancing sales rate and sales price

Making the Right Combination of Choices with Research

Making the right combination of choices reminds me of a night years ago, as I was packing for a trip. I hadn't used my suitcase for a long time and I'd forgotten the simple three-digit combination. After some early panic and frustration, I decided I'd just have to crack the code on my own.

I sat in front of the TV and tried different combinations ... "000", "001", "002", you get the picture. Extremely tedious. I was pleasantly surprised that after only thirty-five minutes of methodical attempts, I cracked the code. (Okay, I say "only" thirty-five minutes, but it seemed like eternity to me.) The combination was "305", which happened to be my apartment number. (I then clearly remembered that I wanted to pick a code that I'd be sure to remember later. What better than my apartment number?)

On eBay, we're doing kind of the same thing. We want to find the code that unlocks the key to finding a buyer for every listing that is willing to pay the very highest price for each item we sell. If only we knew how to "crack the code" that would tell us exactly what eBay buyers always want.

That's where eBay research comes in. As you already know, selling more listings and getting higher selling prices is not just good luck.

There are always reasons why one listing performs well while others fail. Sometimes it's the day and time the listing ends. Sometimes it's the listing type. Maybe it's the keywords used in the title, the starting price, the category, or dozens of other listing choices. But, of course, it's never that simple. It's really a combination of all those things. And to make the most money on eBay you have to "crack that code."

Three Selling Strategies

Sales methods are based on three strategies:

1. High Volume (or LSR)
   Strategy: A higher volume of sales yields greater profit in the long run, even if the profit-per-listing is less. Great for bulk items.
2. High Profit Per Listing (or ASP)
   Strategy: A greater profit per sale yields greater overall profit in the long-run, even if the conversion rate is lower. Great for unique or less common items.

3. Balance: LSR x ASP

    Strategy: This plan tries to strike a balance between increasing conversion rate and earning more per sale in order to get the greatest profit in the long run. Great for selling common items at non-bulk rates.

The image below gives a quick reference for finding answers in your research about how to increase volume and boost your profit per listing.

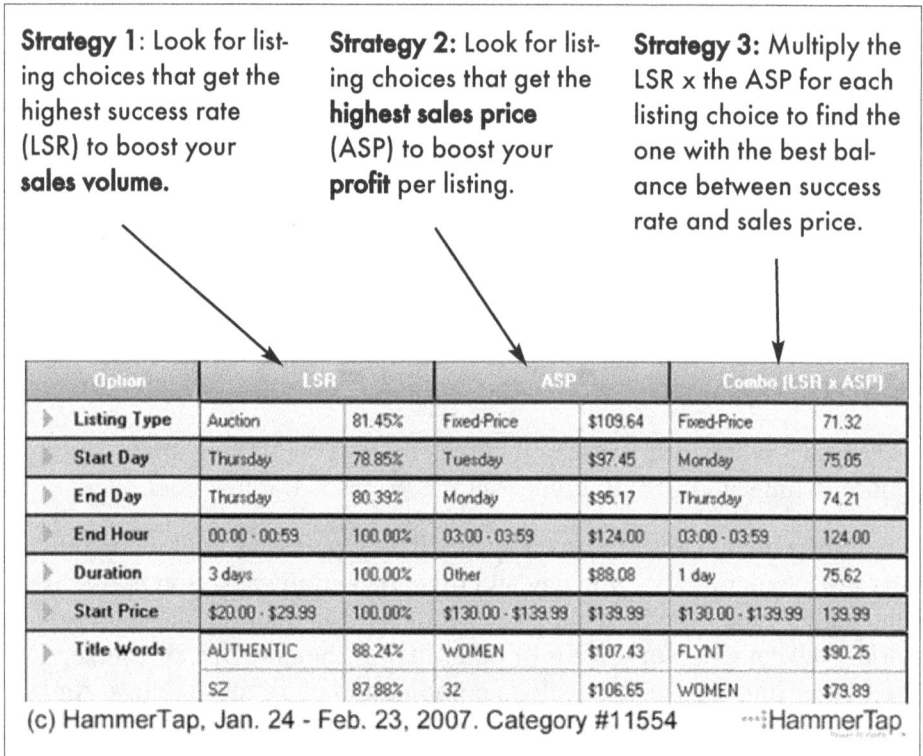

Strategy 1: Look for listing choices that get the highest success rate (LSR) to boost your **sales volume.**

Strategy 2: Look for listing choices that get the **highest sales price** (ASP) to boost your **profit** per listing.

Strategy 3: Multiply the LSR x the ASP for each listing choice to find the one with the best balance between success rate and sales price.

Option	LSR		ASP		Combo (LSR x ASP)	
Listing Type	Auction	81.45%	Fixed-Price	$109.64	Fixed-Price	71.32
Start Day	Thursday	78.85%	Tuesday	$97.45	Monday	75.05
End Day	Thursday	80.39%	Monday	$95.17	Thursday	74.21
End Hour	00:00 - 00:59	100.00%	03:00 - 03:59	$124.00	03:00 - 03:59	124.00
Duration	3 days	100.00%	Other	$88.08	1 day	75.62
Start Price	$20.00 - $29.99	100.00%	$130.00 - $139.99	$139.99	$130.00 - $139.99	139.99
Title Words	AUTHENTIC	88.24%	WOMEN	$107.43	FLYNT	$90.25
	SZ	87.88%	32	$106.65	WOMEN	$79.89

(c) HammerTap, Jan. 24 - Feb. 23, 2007. Category #11554   HammerTap

Figure 12.1: Selling Optimization Strategies for 7 for All Mankind and NYD Jeans

    The table above shows recommended optimizations for each of our three strategies. Items in the LSR column are the listing choices that, statistically speaking, will give you the best chances to sell. Items in the ASP column are listing choices that will give you the highest profit per sale. And the Combo column tells you which listing decisions to make to get the best balance between the two.

Every research tool shows this information in a different way. But these are the three types of information you should be looking for—no matter what tool you are using.

Let's take a closer look at each strategy.

Strategy 1: Selling a Higher Volume

We've talked a lot about LSR (Listing Success Rate) throughout this book. But, so far, we've only looked at it in a general way. Now we're going to look at it in a very specific way.

If you remember, in Chapter 3, we identified 7 for All Mankind, NYD jeans as a "hot" product. Let's say you bought five hundred pair. You bought that many because at that volume, you could get the deep discount.

But, you know there's a risk here. The problem with listing such a high volume is that the market will become a little more saturated. (Remember our lesson on supply and demand in Chapter 4?) This means you'll probably have to sell each pair for a little less than you would if there weren't so many pairs of the jeans available on the market at the same time.

With this strategy, even though you'll be selling each pair of jeans for a little less, it's okay. You've run the numbers and found that you can make more money, in the long-run, if you sell more jeans at a lower price.

The question is, how are you going to increase the number of jeans you sell? How are you going to sell a higher volume?

Following is the overall LSR for 7 for All Mankind, NYD jeans. These numbers are important because you will use them as a "measuring stick" to compare your listing choices against.

Analysis Tip: Compare to the Overall LSR

Always compare the LSR (Listing Success Rate) for any listing decision against the overall LSR. For example, if the overall LSR is 72% and the LSR for regular auctions without BIN is 81%, then you know that your listing choice will help you sell more listings.

Results		Listing Success Rate (LSR)
Total Listings	508	
Listings with Sale	368	
Listing Success Rate (LSR)	**72.44%**	
Average Sales Price (ASP)	$90.22	
Total Sales	$33,200.50	
Sellers with Sale	123	
Average Sales Per Seller	2.99	
Average Revenue Per Seller	$269.92	

72.44 %

27.56 %

☐ Listings With Sale
☐ Listings W/Out Sale

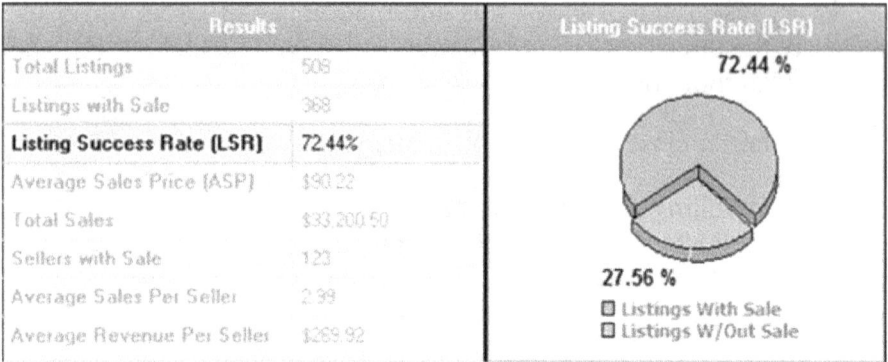

(c) HammerTap, Jan. 24 - Feb. 23, 2007. Category #11554   ⋯⋮HammerTap

Figure 12.2: Overall LSR is 72.44%

The figure above shows us that the overall success rate for this item is 72.44%. Now we're going to find out what ways we can list this product to increase our chances of selling it.

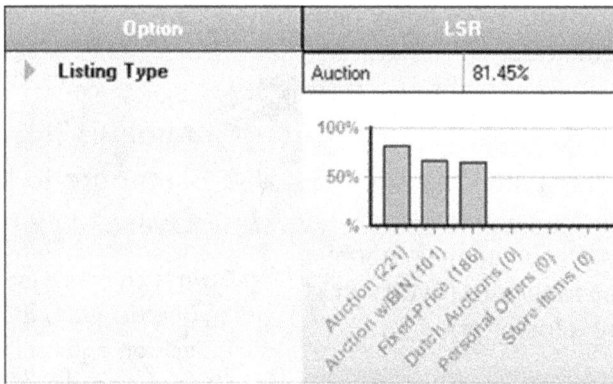

Option	LSR	
▶ **Listing Type**	Auction	81.45%

100%
50%
%

Auction (221)
Auction w/BIN (101)
Fixed Price (186)
Dutch Auctions (0)
Personal Offers (0)
Store Items (0)

(c) HammerTap, Jan. 24 - Feb. 23, 2007   ⋯⋮HammerTap

Figure 12.3: Auction without BIN LSR is 81%

Figure 12.3 shows us that, of all the listing types, regular auctions without BIN (Buy It Now) had the highest success rate (LSR). Regular auctions sold 81% of the time, while the overall average was 72% (see Figure 12.2).

This means that regular auctions will give us a 9% boost in conversion, helping us sell a higher volume over time.

Let's look at another example—ending time. Below is a table that shows the success rate for each hour of the day:

In Figure 12.4, we see a definite window of time that is best to end these listings to boost the conversion rate for our jeans. We can increase the conversion rate from the overall 72% to between 83% and 92% just by changing the time that we end our listing!

There were other times that appeared to work wonderfully, but weren't based on enough data to be sure. For example, 95% of the twenty-one listings that ended between 1 PM (13:00) to 2 PM (14:00), Pacific Time sold.

100% of listings that sold between 10 PM (22:00) and 11 PM (23:00) sold. But, don't get excited yet. There were only nine listings that sold that hour. It might be valid, but we don't know for sure because there weren't enough listings. You want your listing decisions to be solid, and based on evidence, or else you're just back at the guessing game.

Item Description	Number of Auctions	Auction Success Rate
Ending Time		
00:00 - 00:59	8	100.00%
01:00 - 01:59	3	100.00%
02:00 - 02:59	5	80.00%
03:00 - 03:59	2	100.00%
04:00 - 04:59	0	0.00%
05:00 - 05:59	5	80.00%
06:00 - 06:59	5	20.00%
07:00 - 07:59	8	75.00%
08:00 - 08:59	9	77.78%
09:00 - 09:59	16	62.50%
10:00 - 10:59	33	57.58%
11:00 - 11:59	33	72.73%
12:00 - 12:59	30	83.33%
13:00 - 13:59	21	95.24%
14:00 - 14:59	18	83.33%
15:00 - 15:59	14	92.86%
16:00 - 16:59	21	85.71%
17:00 - 17:59	13	92.31%
18:00 - 18:59	30	56.67%
19:00 - 19:59	78	50.00%
20:00 - 20:59	110	75.45%
21:00 - 21:59	30	80.00%
22:00 - 22:59	9	100.00%
23:00 - 23:59	7	71.43%

(c) 2007 ⋯HammerTap

Figure 12.4: Best Hour to End (Jan. 24 – Feb. 23, 2007)

Questions to Answer When Boosting Your Success Rate

You can increase your listing success rate in so many other ways, such as start and end day, title words, duration, start price, and listing features. And you'll use the same techniques I've outlined above to discover how.

Here are some specific questions you need to answer with research, to help you maximize your success rate:

- **Listing Type:** What type of listing will attract more buyers?
- **Starting Day:** Which day should I begin my listing to attract more buyers? (This information is particularly helpful if the Listing Type you are going to run is a regular auction with Buy It Now. These listings could end at any time, but you have control over the start day here. This gives you great info about your buyers' habits.)
- **Ending Day:** On which day are most buyers of this product doing their actual purchasing (as opposed to watching)?
- **Duration:** How long should I list my item to create urgency to buy? (Remember, the goal here is to make more sales.)
- **Start Price:** Which starting price will stimulate more bids and attract more buyers?
- **Title Words:** Which title words attract the most buyers?
- **Listing Features:** Which listing features will give me the best visibility?

Don't Forget to Account for ASP

Even though the focus for this strategy is to find ways to sell more often, be careful not to discount the effect of your choices on the selling price. While you will most likely have to sacrifice some of your selling price per listing with this strategy, you want to make sure that you don't make too big of a sacrifice. You'll see what I mean on the next page:

Cowie & Cano

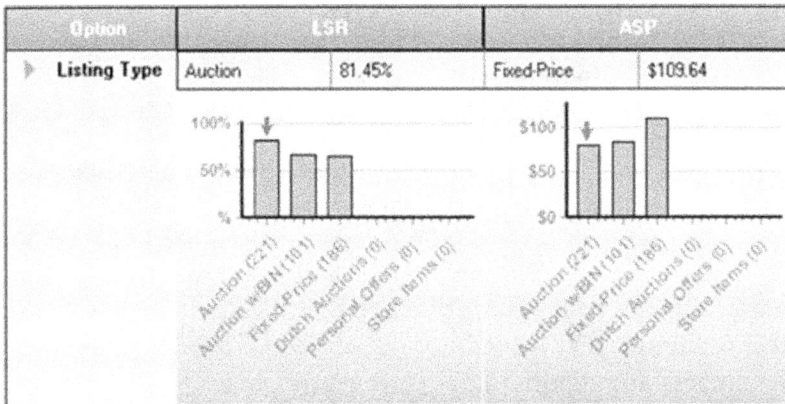

Option	LSR		ASP	
Listing Type	Auction	81.45%	Fixed-Price	$109.64

(c)HammerTap. Jan. 24 - Feb. 23, 2007. Category #11554 ····HammerTap

Figure 12.5: Compare Listing Performance with LSR Against ASP

Let's use the information in the figure above to decide if gaining the extra boost in sales rate is going to force me to sacrifice more than I want to with my selling price. Look at the graph with LSR at the top of the box (in Figure 12.5). It shows that regular auctions without BIN (Buy It Now) have the best success rate: 81%.

But, look at the graph with ASP at the top of the box (also in Figure 12.5). It shows that the average selling price for regular listings without BIN are selling for around $75. That's $15 less than the overall average selling price for this item. (See Figure 12.2).

Your decision about whether the sacrifice is too great depends on:
- whether you can still make a profit at that price point ($75 in the case above)
- whether the profit on your sales price will still help you make more money in the long run

Strategy 2: Making More Money Per Sale

This strategy focuses on whether you will make more money in the long run if you concentrate on making the most money possible with each sale.

Just as with Strategy 1 (which focuses on selling more often), this strategy also has its sacrifices. This time, you'll risk making fewer sales over time. But, if you can make more money over time by selling at a higher price, even if it means fewer sales, this is the strategy for you.

But where do you begin?

You remember the drill. The research method is going to be exactly the same as with Strategy 1. But, this time, your focus will be on ASP (Average Sales Price) instead of LSR.

Below is the overall ASP for 7 for All Mankind, NYD jeans. These numbers are important because you will use them as a "measuring stick" to compare your listing choices against.

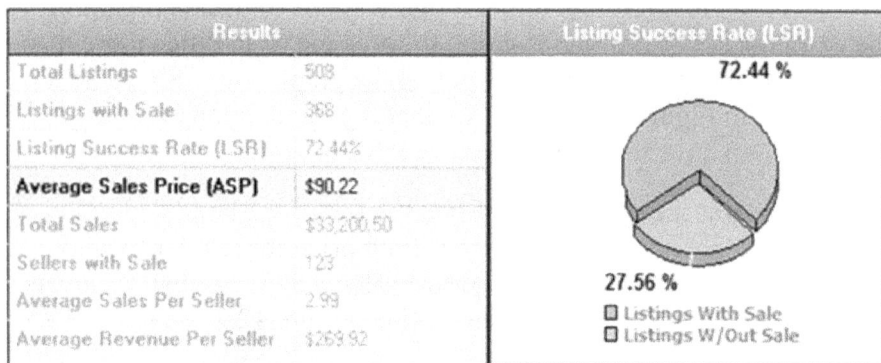

Results		Listing Success Rate (LSR)
Total Listings	508	72.44 %
Listings with Sale	368	
Listing Success Rate (LSR)	72.44%	
Average Sales Price (ASP)	**$90.22**	
Total Sales	$33,200.50	
Sellers with Sale	123	27.56 %
Average Sales Per Seller	2.99	☐ Listings With Sale
Average Revenue Per Seller	$269.92	☐ Listings W/Out Sale

(c)HammerTap, Jan. 24 - Feb. 23, 2007. Category #11554 ⋯ HammerTap

Figure 12.6: Overall ASP is $90.22.

The figure above shows us that the overall average selling price for this item is $90.22. Now we're going to find out what ways we can list this product to increase the selling price.

The research chart on the next page shows us that, of all the listing types, fixed price had the highest price per sale. Fixed price listings sold for almost $110, while the overall average was around $90 (see Figure 12.6).

Option	ASP	
▷ **Listing Type**	Fixed-Price	$109.64

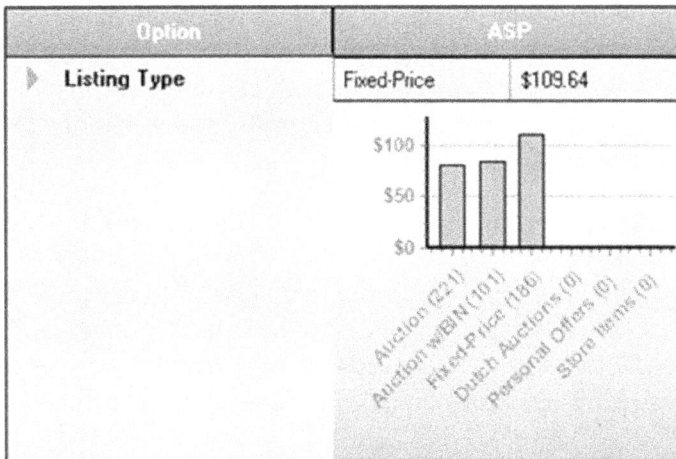

(c) HammerTap, Jan. 24 - Feb. 23, 2007   ┄HammerTap

This means that fixed price listings could boost the selling price by $20.

Let's look at another example—ending time. Below is a table that shows the average selling prices for each hour of the day:

Item Description	Number of Auctions	ASP per Item
Ending Time		
00:00 - 00:59	8	$83.37
01:00 - 01:59	3	$94.66
02:00 - 02:59	5	$119.50
03:00 - 03:59	2	$124.00
04:00 - 04:59	0	$0.00
05:00 - 05:59	4	$110.25
06:00 - 06:59	5	$119.00
07:00 - 07:59	5	$112.50
08:00 - 08:59	9	$85.31
09:00 - 09:59	16	$101.95
10:00 - 10:59	33	$98.24
11:00 - 11:59	33	$99.62
12:00 - 12:59	30	$80.33
13:00 - 13:59	21	$97.27
14:00 - 14:59	18	$99.31
15:00 - 15:59	14	$76.09
16:00 - 16:59	21	$77.50
17:00 - 17:59	13	$68.00
18:00 - 18:59	30	$83.17
19:00 - 19:59	28	$90.77
20:00 - 20:59	110	$99.93
21:00 - 21:59	30	$89.50
22:00 - 22:59	9	$93.39
23:00 - 23:59	7	$72.50

(c) 2007   ┄HammerTap

Analysis Tip: Stick to Your Strategy

Notice that the best listing type to get the highest success rate (Figure 12.3) is different than the best listing type to get the best sales price per listing (Figure 12.7). This is often the case and varies by item, brand, style, and etc. Because they are so often different, it's important for you to research every item, and to research according to the selling strategy you've chosen for that product.

Figure 12.8: Best Hour to End
(Jan. 24 – Feb. 23, 2007)

In the previous chart, we see a block of time between 9 AM and 3 PM that has proven to be the best time to end in order to get the best price. There were other hours that had equally great results, or better in some cases; but they weren't based on quite enough listings to justify betting the farm on those hours.

For example, from 11 AM to 12 PM (Pacific Time), thirty-three listings ended at an average selling price of $101.95. At 7 AM, we see an average selling price of $112, but that's based on only nine listings. The number of listings is small enough that this might be a fluke, or some other factor may have caused the spike in sales price. Again, you want to base your decisions on solid evidence, and not flukes.

Questions to Answer When Boosting Your Sales Price

You can increase your sales price in so many other ways, such as start and end day, title words, duration, start price, and listing features. And you'll use the same techniques I've outlined above to discover how.

Here are some specific questions you need to answer with research, to help you maximize your sales price per listing:

- **Listing Type:** What type of listing will attract higher-paying buyers?
- **Starting Day:** Which day should I begin my listing to attract higher-paying buyers? (This information is particularly helpful if the listing type you are going to run is a regular auction with Buy It Now.)
- **Ending Day:** On which day are the highest-paying buyers of this product doing their actual purchasing (as opposed to watching)?
- **Duration:** How long should I list my item to attract higher-paying buyers? (Remember, the goal here is to make more money per sale.)
- **Start Price:** Which starting price will attract higher-paying buyers?
- **Title Words:** Which title words will get more attention from higher-paying buyers?
- **Listing Features:** Which listing features will give me the best visibility?

Don't Forget to Account for LSR

Even though the focus for this strategy is to find ways to increase your selling price (ASP), be careful not to discount the effect of your choices on the sell-through rate (LSR).

While you will most likely have to sacrifice a little on your success rate with this strategy, you want to make sure that you don't make too big of a sacrifice. Here's what I mean:

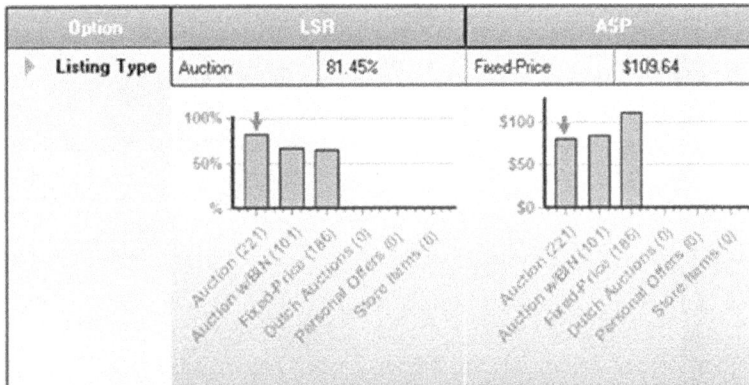

(c)HammerTap, Jan. 24 - Feb. 23, 2007. Category #11554 ⋯HammerTap

Figure 12.9: Compare Listing Performance with ASP Against LSR

Let's use the figure above to help decide if earning more money from each sale (ASP) is going to end up making me close too few sales. Look at the graph with ASP at the top of the box (in Figure 12.9). It shows that fixed price listings sell for $109 on average.

But, look at the graph with LSR at the top of the box (also in Figure 12.9). It shows that the success rate for fixed price listings is around 65%. That's about 7% less than the overall success rate for this item. (See Figure 12.2).

Your decision about whether the sacrifice is too great depends on whether you can still make enough sales to make more money in the long run.

Strategy 3: Striking a Balance Between Volume and Price

This is the road most sellers will use at one time or another. This strategy is for the item that:

- you didn't buy at a bulk rate, so you have to **focus on sales price** (ASP)
- is common enough on the marketplace that there is a lot of competition, so you have to also **focus on increasing your chances of selling** (LSR)

In other words, we want to go "up and to the right!"

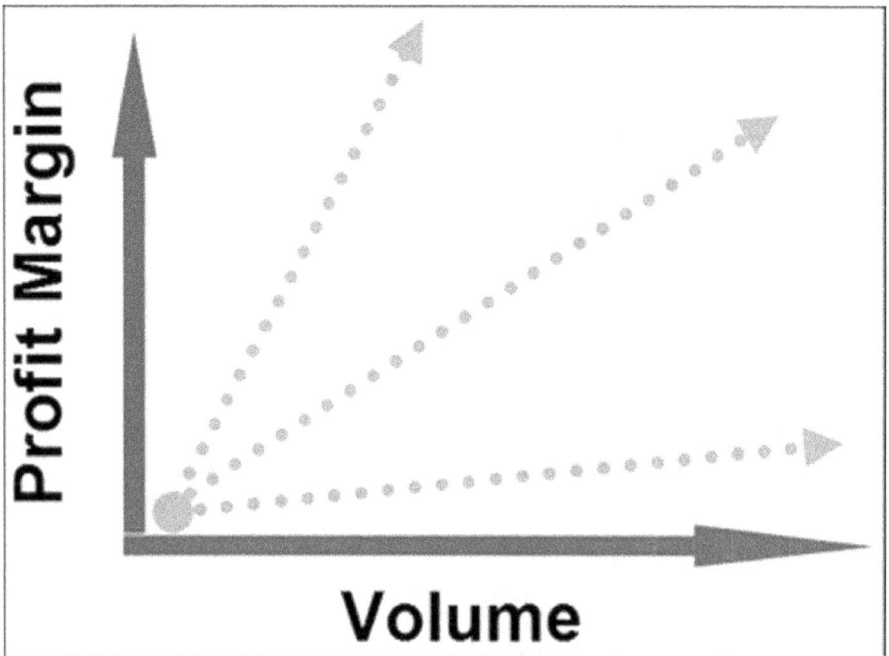

Figure 12.10: Balancing High Volume with High Profit

But how do you get up and to the right? How do you strike a balance between LSR and ASP? Let me show you. It's just as simple as the last two strategies.

Below is the overall LSR and ASP for 7 for All Mankind, NYD jeans. These numbers are important because you will use them as a "measuring stick" to compare your listing choices against.

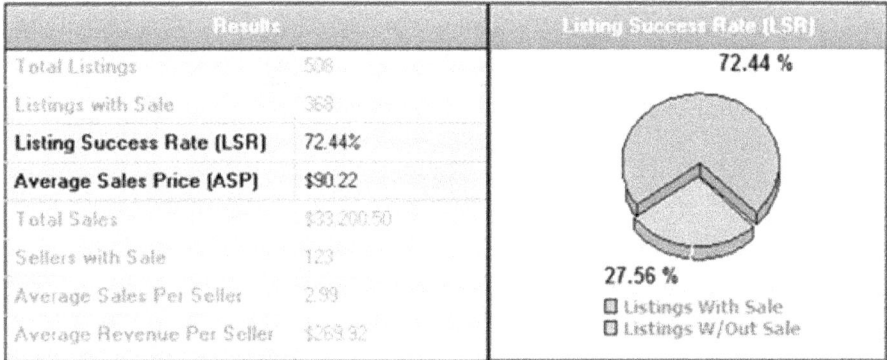

Results		Listing Success Rate (LSR)
Total Listings	508	72.44 %
Listings with Sale	368	
Listing Success Rate (LSR)	72.44%	
Average Sales Price (ASP)	$90.22	
Total Sales	$33,200.50	
Sellers with Sale	123	27.56 %
Average Sales Per Seller	2.99	☐ Listings With Sale
Average Revenue Per Seller	$269.32	☐ Listings W/Out Sale

(c) HammerTap, Jan. 24 - Feb. 23, 2007   ⋯HammerTap

Figure 12.11: Overall LSR and ASP

The figure above shows us that the overall success rate for this item is 72.44% and the overall average selling price is $90.22. Now we're going to find out how we can optimize the listings for this product in a way that gives us a great selling price and a better chance of selling.

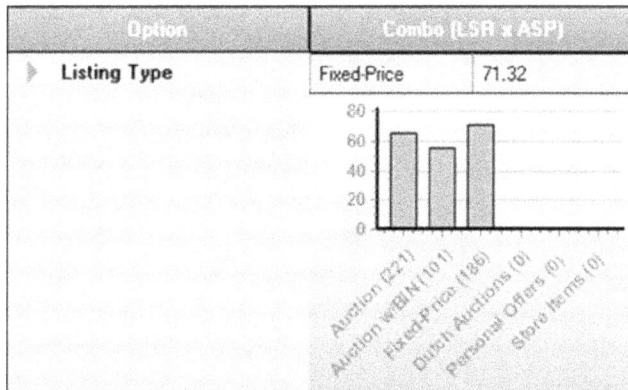

Figure 12.12:
Fixed Price Yields the
Best Balance

Option	Combo (LSR x ASP)	
▶ **Listing Type**	Fixed-Price	71.32

(c) HammerTap, Jan. 24 - Feb. 23, 2007   ⋯HammerTap

Figure 12.12 shows us that, of all the listing types, fixed price listings give us the best balance between LSR and ASP. Fixed price listings will help us move up and to the right.

Let's compare the LSR, ASP, and combo information for fixed price listings. The graphs below let us compare how fixed price listings performed according to LSR, ASP, and combo (our balance).

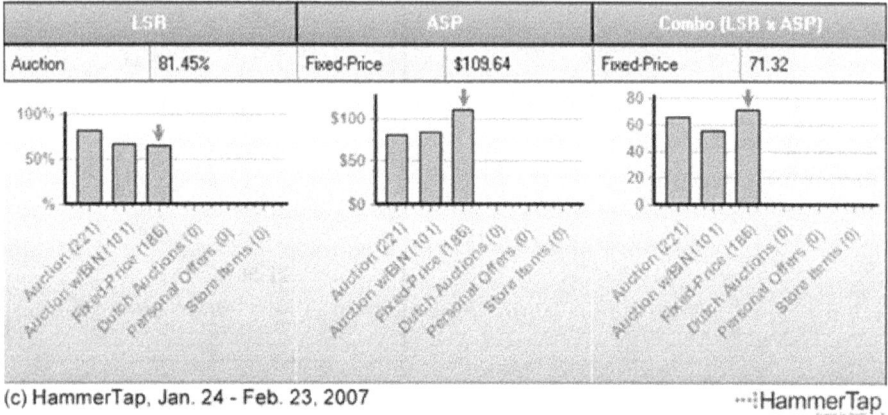

(c) HammerTap, Jan. 24 - Feb. 23, 2007   ····HammerTap

Figure 12.13: LSR, ASP, and Combo Compared

According to the research, fixed price listings sold around 65% of the time for $109. But what makes fixed price listings the best choice? It has the best combo value. What's the combo value? I'm glad you asked.

Combo Value Formula: LSR x ASP = Combo Value
Example: $109 x 65% = $71.32

Here's the best part of this entire chapter. The combo value tells you how much every single fixed price listing made, on average. Notice I didn't say every sale. This is every listing, win or fail. All the listings average about $71 each. Amazing!

Choosing the Right Strategy

The right strategy really depends on your needs.

- If you want to sell the highest possible volume, make the listing choices with the highest LSR.
- If you want to make the most profit possible for each sale, make the listing choices with the highest ASP.
- If you want to get a balance between the two (a majority of sellers and products fall into this category), make the listing choices with the highest combo value.

You may not have known that you have so many listing choices. But, take comfort in knowing that you will never again need to guess how to list your products to get the most profit over time.

Grow My Profits Study Example

Grow My Profits study participant Tim Reynolds increased his eBay revenues by more than 40% using the strategies learned in this chapter. Read an excerpt from his business journal below:

"HammerTap has helped me to determine what to cutback on, what to increase and what time of day and week to list. HammerTap has also given insight into what special features and keywords to use in my listings. This has increased my margins (on some products by as much as 30%) and decreased my fees. Because I have been able to cut back on the number of auctions I am managing, I have had more time to research product life cycle, new products, and my competition."

And this is what we're after with research! Spending the most time on the things that make the most profit. Tim's made a science out of figuring out exactly how and when his buyers are searching for his product, and exactly what attracts them.

And you can, too!

Highlights:

- Tim learned how and when to offer his listings to eBay buyers using the same methods taught in this chapter.
- By learning what the buyer expected and wanted, Tim's business grew dramatically over the course of the study.

Product Expansion Schedule

13

Over the four years I have been directly involved with the eBay community, I have met some amazing people. The most successful sellers all had one thing in common: passion.

They love what they do. Looking over this book, I've noticed that we've given a ton of technical theories and physical examples. We've talked about a lot of proven techniques that help drive profits. But don't loose sight of the fact that while an eBay business can be very profitable, it is not a job.

An eBay business is the epitome of what it means to be an entrepreneur. The fact that so many people succeed on eBay and make an excellent living is a real testimony to the human spirit of determination and capitalism. Congratulate yourself! You really are in one of the greatest businesses on the planet.

I know exactly what you mean, Robin. When it comes to taking hold of your own future to get what you want, even kids seem to have that entrepreneurial spirit (try spelling that ten times fast!).

The summer when I was seven, our family lived in a little town called Henrietta Oklahoma. And the most exciting event of every day was when the ice-cream truck would roll through town, right in front of our house.

We didn't get an allowance, as kids, and my mom rarely gave us money to get ice-cream. So, we had to be a little inventive when it came to getting ice-cream money. I remember rummaging through the garage or the attic or old toy chests to find things we could sell door-to-door. It was our very own microcosm of an eBay environment. And, after time, we got pretty good at it. We learned which phrases to use to close the sale and earn a few more pennies.

You probably had a similar experience with a lemonade stand or some other similar project, right?

We're not kids anymore. And we're not working for pennies, nickels, and dimes. But, that awakening and need to direct our own financial future had to start somewhere. Earning ice-cream money was our ambition as kids. And we used that ambition, and the tools at hand, to get the ice-cream.

Now is when your ambition, that passion that Robin was talking about, comes in. It's the driving force behind your expansion schedule. Ready to take on the world?

During this chapter, Jen tells you how to build a product expansion schedule:

Step 1: Plan the work
Step 2: Take inventory of your current opportunities
Step 3: Plug current opportunities into your schedule
Step 4: Work your plan

Remember the Turnover Principle

Remember the Turnover Principle in Chapter 2? The product expansion schedule you are about to create is directly related to that principle. You remember: 1, 2, 3. Research, source, sell. Repeat.

In the Turnover Principle, the goal is to have products in all three stages of the cycle all the time. This cycle is the basis—the framework—for your product expansion schedule.

As we said in Chapter 2, designing your selling efforts this way gives you greater control over your business to:

- **Focus on Profit:** You'll focus your attention on executing a flexible plan, rather than on reacting to unanticipated challenges. This means you can spend a majority of your time on products that make a profit.

- **Stay In Demand All the Time:** You'll have in-demand products on the market all the time because as you phase items out, you'll also phase new items in.
- **Stay Ahead of Change:** Instead of being caught off guard with changes in demand, you'll know how to predict change and produce offerings your buyers want, when they want it.

Step 1: Plan the Work

Most eBay sellers I've spoken with want to expand their businesses. They want to learn how to sell what they've got—well and efficiently. Then, they really want to expand their product offerings. Someday. It's a goal.

In reality, without a detailed plan, few sellers actually take their businesses any further. Any luck they experience quickly vanishes because the eBay environment changes so quickly.

That's why your expansion plan begins with some clear and specific goals. Here are a few questions to help you get started:

What Do You Want to accomplish?

List three very clear goals.

Examples: "I want to have twenty-five solid, profitable products selling regularly on eBay." Or, "I want to become a Gold PowerSeller." Or, "I want to increase my overall success rate to 50%."

How Close are You to Each Goal?

Examples: "I need to find fifteen more profitable products." Or, "I'm selling $5,500 per month. This means I need to increase my monthly sales another $4,500." Or, "I have some products that are selling 50% of the time or better. I need to add more products with a high success rate."

What are Some Ways You Plan to Accomplish Your Goals?

Examples: "I'm going to spend thirty minutes/day researching new products until I have my new product candidates. Then, I'm going to spend one hour/day finding sources for those products until I am ready to offer the new products." Or "To raise more revenue, I can find more profitable products to sell and I can also research ways to make more money on the items I'm already selling." Or "I can evaluate the products I have right now to see how I might be able to increase the success rates. I can also research and find sources for new products with higher success rates."

When Do You Want to Reach Some of the Milestones Toward Accomplishing Your Goals?

Examples: "Date (three months from now): I will be selling fifteen more profitable products." Or "Date (four months from now): I will become a Gold PowerSeller." Or "Date (three months from now): I will have an average success rate of 50% or higher."

> **Tip: Reaching Your Goals is a Process, Not an Event**
> Keep in mind that reaching your goals is not an event. Because this is an ever-changing market, you will need to maintain your efforts.

Before you complete each step in the rest of this process, you should refer back to these goals. This way, you'll make sure all your efforts move you toward accomplishing them

Step 2: Take Inventory of Your Current Opportunities

Now that you've outlined your goals, you're ready to begin building your product expansion schedule. The next step in creating your schedule is to take inventory of your current opportunities.

Divide you opportunities (or products) into four categories:

- **Ideas**—These are products you have been thinking about selling or have been curious about, but that you haven't done any research for.
- **Researching**—These are products you are investigating right now.
- **Sourcing**—These are products you are trying to find a source for.
- **Selling**—These are products you are selling right now.

Step 3: Plug Current Opportunities into Your Expansion Schedule

The Product Expansion Schedule is a series of four lists (corresponding to the categories in Step 2). We've created those lists for you at the end of this chapter. Begin placing your products and ideas from Step 2 on the appropriate list.

Ideas List	Not every product on this list will make it to the Researching list. This is a brainstorm. Write the projected date for beginning research on it. Also, mark whether the product is a seasonal item, an item you've sold before and want to sell again, or an upcoming (new) model of a product you are already selling. Items in this list come from: • new product ideas (see Chapter 3) • seasonal items not in season • new models that will replace a model of a product you are currently selling (e.g., a new set of your brand of golf clubs is going to come out next year)
Researching List	This is the first step toward narrowing your brainstorming list. Not every product in this list will progress to the Sourcing list. Write the projected date that you will move the product out of this list. Also, mark whether you are re-evaluating a product you are currently selling (because demand for it has changed). Research on the product should give you information about timing and when would be a target date for you begin selling the item. Items in this list come from: • items from your "Contemplating" list • items from your "Selling" list that you need to re-evaluate
Sourcing List	This is the next step toward narrowing your brainstorming list. Write the projected date that you will begin selling the item. Also, when you add a product to this list, mark whether this is a new item or an item you want to renegotiate.

Sourcing List cont.	The date you plan to begin selling a product will rely on when you will have funds to purchase the item. Items in this list come from: • items you've just finished researching • items from your "Selling" list that you want to renegotiate
Selling List	When you add products to this list, mark whether they are seasonal or if a new model will enter the market within the next few months to take its place. For optimal performance, items in this list must have gone through both the research and sourcing lists. Even if this is a seasonal product that you've sold before, you should do the research again before you purchase more of the product or sell it again. The market is constantly changing, and because of this, your selling strategy will need to change.

Tip: Use a Spreadsheet for Your Expansion Schedule
You could easily create a spreadsheet to store the information on these lists. The lists at the end of this chapter are examples for your convenience.

Step 4: Now Work the Plan
You've got your plan, now work it.

1. Compare your goals to your product expansion schedule often so that you will stay focused.
2. Systematically review the lists you created (Ideas, Research, Source, and Sell) and do the work to move items from one list to the next.

For example, you should work to move items in the Ideas list to the Researching list. Move items in the Researching list to the Sourcing list, and etc.

The process looks like this:

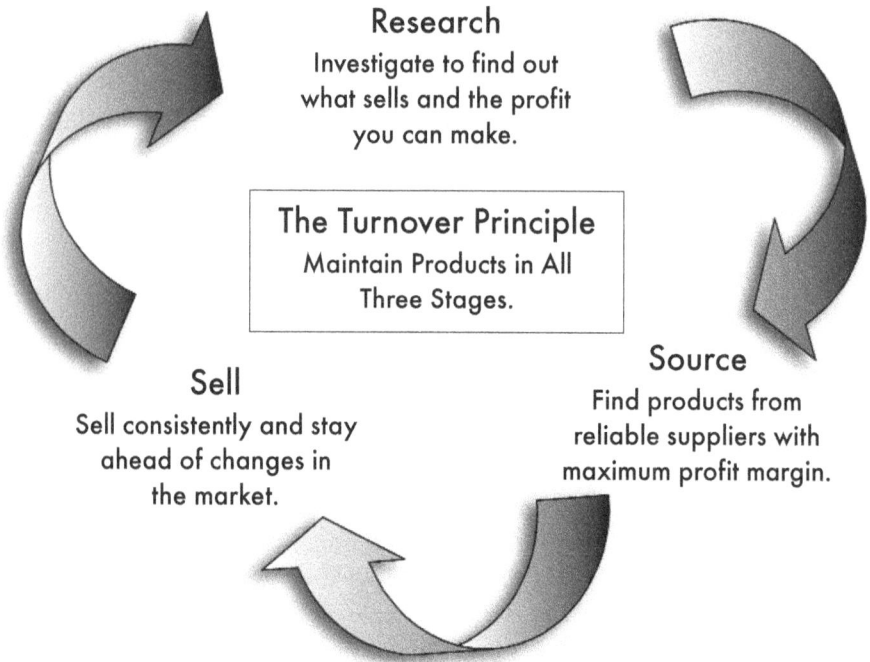

Research
Investigate to find out
what sells and the profit
you can make.

The Turnover Principle
Maintain Products in All
Three Stages.

Sell
Sell consistently and stay
ahead of changes in
the market.

Source
Find products from
reliable suppliers with
maximum profit margin.

Figure 13.1: The Turnover Principle

With the Product Expansion schedule, you've designed a clear path to accomplish your selling goals. Little setbacks will happen. But so will bursts of over-achievement. Overall, if you work steadily and stick to the plan, you will grow your business through smarter choices—not harder work.

In the end, your products will give a **fantastic eBay performance**.

Grow My Profits Study Example

Somewhere toward the end of the Grow My Profits study, I asked our participants a question I'd been a little afraid of. The participants had gotten fairly deep into the research and had made research part of the routine of running their businesses. Most of them didn't make sourcing or selling decisions anymore without the research.

So, I asked the question, closing my eyes and crossing my fingers: "Is research taking up too much of your time? Is it distracting you from other important aspects of your business?"

The response was unanimous. Each participant said that not only was research helping them generate more revenue, but they were actually saving time. Why?

They no longer wasted time on ventures that didn't work. They focused on efforts that brought in money. And, best of all, now they had time to begin expanding their businesses.

What did "expanding" mean? It meant aggressively sourcing products, using solutions like Worldwide Brands and selling them with confidence on multiple marketplaces.

We developed the Product Expansion Schedule based on what we learned from businesses in our study.

(Source: Grow My Profits by HammerTap, www.hammertap.com/growmyprofits, and Worldwide Brands, www.worldwidebrands.com)

My Product Expansion Schedule

My Goals

Goals:

1. _____
   _____
2. _____
   _____
3. _____

What I need to reach my goals:

1. _____
   _____
2. _____
   _____
3. _____

How I'm going to accomplish my goals:

1. _____
   _____
2. _____
   _____
3. _____

Target Dates:

Date: _____; Milestone: _____

_____

Date: _____; Milestone: _____

_____

Date: _____; Milestone: _____

_____

My Current Opportunities			
Contemplating	Researching	Sourcing	Selling

My Ideas List

- Date = Day you'll begin researching and move the item to your research list.
- Seasonal = A seasonal item you may or may not have sold before.
- Sold Before = An item you have sold before and are not currently selling.
- New Model = A new, upcoming model of a product you currently sell.

Product	Date	Seasonal?	Sold Before?	New Model?

My Research List
- Date = Day you'll move the item to your sourcing list and begin sourcing it.
- Re-Evaluating = An item you have sold but stopped for re-evaluation.
- Reason = The reason you are re-evaluating the item.

Product	Date	Reevaluating?	Reason?

My Sourcing List

- Date = Day you'll begin move the item to you Sell list and begin selling.
- Renegotiate = An item for which you want to renegotiate your sourcing contract.
- Sold Before = An item you have sold before and are not currently selling.
- Funds Needed = Funds you need to raise to purchase the product.

Product	Date	Renegotiate	Why?	Funds Needed

My Selling List
- Seasonal = Indicates the item is a seasonal item.
- New Model Coming = Indicates a new model for the current
    product is coming.
- End Date = The date you will stop selling a seasonal item or old model.

Product	Seasonal?	New Model Coming?	End Date

About the Authors

ROBIN COWIE, President, www.World-wideBrands.com, is an Internet entrepreneur, filmmaker and television producer. One of the producers of *The Blair Witch Project*, he is the recipient of the Nova Award from the Producers Guild of America, the Independent Spirit Award from the Independent Feature Project, the Prix de Jeuvenes from the Cannes Film Festival, and the Professional Achievement Award from the University of Central Florida. His latest film project, *Altered*, was recently released by Rogue Pictures.

Cowie has been the principal executive in three start-up businesses. Over the last four years he took Worldwide Brands Inc., an online product sourcing company, from a customer base of around 10,000 people to over 100,000 active internet entrepreneur members. He is the co-host of the Entrepreneur Magazine Product Sourcing radio show, the co-host of the Entrepreneur Magazine eBiz Radio show, and a contributing editor to the eBay Radio show. He has toured with eBay University and been a key speaker at the last four eBay Live conventions.

Born and raised in Durban, South Africa, he is the proud father of two children and continues his entertainment and internet entrepreneurial activities from Orlando, Florida.

JEN CANO, VP Marketing for HammerTap, LLC., has a passion for writing and for helping online business owners understand complex subjects. In her work at HammerTap, she takes a special interest in individual clients, studying their needs to help provide direction for the development of practical and powerful research tools, as well as meaningful educational programs.

Cano, HammerTap's spokeswoman, is an eBay Certified Consultant and is recognized as an eBay market research expert. She currently acts as a contributing editor for eBay Radio, providing weekly reports on "What's Hot on eBay," and creates and hosts monthly workshops for the eBay community. Cano also serves on the content committee for Online Market World (a nationally recognized convention), and speaks at many industry events each year.

Her love for music, cooking, and literature is part of her everyday life with her three children and husband.

Appendix A

Research Formula
Quick Guide

Time Value Formula

Referenced in Chapter 6

(cost of my time per hour)/(# of listings per hour) = my time value
    Example: ($30) / (6) = $5
             My paycheck is **$5 for every sale**.

Maximum Cost Formula

Referenced in Chapter 6

$$\text{Maximum Cost} = \text{ASP} \left[\left(\frac{\text{Insertion Fees}}{\text{LSR}} \right) + \text{CODB} + \text{Time Value} \right]$$

    Example: LSR: 94.64%
               ASP: $47.62
               Insertion Fees: $.75
               Costs of Doing Business: $5.12
               My Time Value per Listing: $5

$$\$47.62 - \left[\left(\frac{\$.75}{94.64\%} \right) + \$5.12 + 5 \right] = \$36.71$$

The most I can pay for this item, and still be able to pay all my fees (and myself) is $36.71.

Combo Value Formula

Referenced in Chapter 12

               LSR x ASP = Combo Value
    Example: Auction without BIN: $75 x 81% = $60.75
               Auction with BIN: $82 x 66% = $54.12
               Fixed-Price: $109 x 65% = $71.32

The listing choice with the highest combo value is Fixed-Price.

Appendix B

Product Sourcing
Scam Report

At Worldwide Brands, we are a fully-staffed product sourcing re-search company that has dedicated the past seven years to finding and qualifying **genuine** wholesale suppliers who are willing to work with home-based Internet business owners. Our experience has taught us that for every **real** wholesale supplier out there, there are dozens of fake "wholesalers" whose main purpose is to separate you from your earnings.

In order to protect yourself from being scammed online when look-ing for products to sell, you **absolutely must know** what to look for. The following are warnings against some common product sourcing hazards we see on the Internet:

Some of these are simply cautions against Internet business offers and practices that, while they may technically be legal, will *never* earn you any money. The only people these programs will ever earn money for are the ones selling them to you.

Please note that the statements made on this page are purely the opinion of Worldwide Brands, Inc., and may or may not be factually validated. We urge you to follow up with your own investigation of the opportunities mentioned below.

Broker Networks

In order to gain the highest possible proceeds on the products you sell online, you must work directly with genuine wholesalers. Any-one who gets in between you and a real, factory-authorized whole-saler is simply turning your order around to someone else, and taking profit that should be yours.

You'll see broker networks advertising as drop shippers and bulk wholesalers. They're not illegal, and they're not scams; but in our ed-ucated opinion, they are also not what they want you to think they are.

Broker networks can best be described as something similar to the multi-level marketing business model. To use their network and access the millions of products they claim you can have drop shipped, you must first *buy* thousands of dollars worth of products yourself—many times from large retail stores. You then become a broker yourself, trying to sell those products to other brokers within the network. You and those other network brokers (people just like you) actually *become* the wholesale suppliers these sites want you to think you're signing up with.

Many times this type of operation will not even process your application unless you can prove you have several thousand dollars to invest in their products, so you can become a broker. Be *very* careful with your credit card information, and ask a *lot* of questions!

This is probably not what you expected from the advertising on their front page, is it? If you're okay with this sort of business model, that's fine. Again, it's not illegal or a scam. Just remember that this is *not* direct wholesale supply in any traditional sense whatsoever.

There are some broker networks that claim to be wholesale suppliers of tens of millions of products. To the best of our knowledge, there is no single wholesale supplier anywhere on the planet that is anywhere near that large. There are also broker networks that claim to be wholesalers of a huge variety of brand name products. But they are simply passing your orders on to other "brokers" just like you, and even retailers of those brand names, and increasing your costs.

To earn the maximum profits on your products, the transactions you make should be between you and a factory-authorized wholesale supplier. Period.

Drop Shippers of "More than 3500 Products"

There are literally thousands of companies out there acting as middlemen for one real drop shipping company. All of those thousands of so-called drop shippers lead back to the same supplier.

I'm talking about a big supplier of imported off-brand merchandise that drop ships directly from their warehouse. They sell some nice products; I actually worked with them a few years ago. Their line consists of about 3,500 widely varying products, mostly decorative figurines, home accents, and giftware. You won't recognize any brand names... it's all imported merchandise, probably mostly from China and the Pacific Rim. We'll call this company "XYZ Wholesalers", for the purpose of this discussion. That's not their real name, of course.

You can sign up with XYZ Wholesalers directly and sell their merchandise on your web site, for a hefty account maintenance fee. I did that a few years ago—however, I no longer work with them. I found the products difficult to sell, for one very good reason. As I said above, they have signed up thousands of people, who are all trying to sell this exact same merchandise on the Internet. That kind of competition, plus the fact that there are already millions of people trying to sell giftware in general on the 'Net, made it impossible for me to make any real money.

Now, here's the problem: along comes Joe Reseller. He signs up with XYZ Wholesalers as a retailer, and has the right to sell their products on the Internet. But he advertises himself as the actual wholesaler. He tells you that he is XYZ Wholesalers, and you can sign up with his web site. He'll drop ship all those products to your customers and make you rich. What he's really doing is sitting in his bedroom in front of his computer, resending your orders to the real XYZ Wholesalers, and driving up your "wholesale" prices.

Lists of Drop Shippers and Bulk Wholesalers for $3

Perhaps you've seen ads like this on an auction site? We have. We buy them. OK, we know we're getting ripped off, but we just have to see them. A few days after paying for them, we get two Xeroxed pages in the mail containing the most worthless information we've ever seen. Or, we get an e-mail that's supposed to be a product sourcing list, or a $15 CD chock full of the same garbage the guy with the $3 list was peddling. If I thought I could make money on the Internet selling wooden birdhouses made in somebody's garage, I'd go into business with my neighbor.

These lists sell for anywhere from $2.50 to about $59. Why do you think they're so cheap? Because nobody had to put any effort into them! It's easy to hit a search engine, type the word "wholesale", throw the first twenty responses on a piece of paper, and sell it for a few bucks. Will it help you earn money? No!

Turn-key Store in a Box

Have you ever come across a "Home Business Opportunity" like this one?

The ad promises to:

- create a storefront for you
- provide you with thousands of products you can drop ship from your store
- provide you with merchant services so you can accept credit cards without having to open a bank account
- give you all this for a one-time price of just $50 (or $149, or $300, etc.)

Wow, doesn't that just sound too good to be true? That's because it is. Oh, sure, they'll do what they say. It's a legal business. But tell me this...just how much money do you think you'll make?

Think about it for a minute… They establish accounts with wholesalers. They mark those wholesale prices *way* up. Then they get you to put in all the time and effort to sell those products, at a very slim profit margin for you. Congratulations! You've just become a commissioned salesman for someone else's business!

Not quite what you had in mind, was it?

Free Wholesale Lists

This is an easy one. Once again... you get what you pay for. No exceptions.

We've checked out these sites. Over and over again, we see them listing companies that we've turned down for inclusion in our own directory. Middlemen, companies that charge large "membership" fees and give you over-inflated price lists in return, companies that require minimum orders in the thousands of dollars, etc. The creators of these sites are simply hoping to get people to click on them so that they can claim high numbers of visitors in order to sell advertising space. We've never seen anything useful on any of these "informational" sites, no matter how many "testimonials" they may list.

For more FREE information about finding **legitimate** wholesale suppliers, go to www.worldwidebrands.com: you can download our e-books, read any of our hundreds of articles, listen to our radio shows, or watch our product sourcing videos.

Appendix C

Coupons

www.ingramcontent.com/pod-product-compliance
Lightning Source LLC
Chambersburg PA
CBHW070402200326
41518CB00011B/2030